Reach Out

Book 3

Reach Out

Book 3

An Anthology of Poems for Schools

Edited by
Thomas Blackburn
and W. T. Cunningham

Nelson

THOMAS NELSON AND SONS LTD
36 Park Street London W1
P.O. Box 336 Apapa Lagos
P.O. Box 25012 Nairobi
P.O. Box 21149 Dar es Salaam
P.O. Box 2187 Accra
77 Coffee Street San Fernando Trinidad

THOMAS NELSON (AUSTRALIA) LTD
597 Little Collins Street Melbourne C1

THOMAS NELSON AND SONS (SOUTH AFRICA)
(PROPRIETARY) LTD
51 Commissioner Street Johannesburg

THOMAS NELSON AND SONS (CANADA) LTD
81 Curlew Drive Don Mills Ontario

THOMAS NELSON AND SONS
Copewood and Davis Streets Camden New Jersey 08103

17 433023 5

Printed in Great Britain by
Western Printing Services Ltd, Bristol

Contents

Part Two

Poetry in School

Unless we have some idea of the relevance of poetry to the business of living it is hard to present it to a class. Even if it is only a question of counting the change, the value of mathematics is obvious enough. Geography tells us about our environment and History illumines the human situation as it stretches back through time. But with poetry there is often uncertainty about what it is and does, and this uncertainty has often led teachers to regard it as a luxury subject (as opposed to the serious business of other subjects of the curriculum). Such a conclusion could not be further from the truth. Maths and Geography are, of course, important but the main direction of our lives is not determined by fact-finding or intellectual exercise; it is determined by deep and hidden energies which are far more difficult to assess.

Poetry is one of the principal languages by which we can explore the human psyche. It gives a local habitation and a name to those strange, often conflicting, powers which overshadow and underlie our daily awareness, and so helps both children and adults to understand them. So of course does psychology, but its terms are often remote and intellectual; mere labels. Poetry not only explores man's inner life but sets out its discoveries in words and images which touch both the mind and heart. Blake wrote, "If the doors of perception were cleansed, everything would appear to man as it is, infinite." Very early on in our lives we tend to black out great swathes of experience; for the sake of comfort and security we choose not to see the infinite and often disturbing significance both of ourselves and the world around us. Poets are people who continue to see and feel with exceptional point and clarity. By reading their works we can enlarge our own vision, and regain a sense of the mystery of "being".

In these books we have introduced poems in twos and threes and small groups, not because they were written by the same person or at the same age, but because in one way or another they are concerned with the same theme. We ourselves have found this method successful both for the obvious value of comparison and because a group can readily form the basis for the work of a period. But there is another important consideration and that is the opportunity provided for extending interest in a theme (when that is natural and spontaneous) into related activities such as personal writing. Poems so grouped tend to "talk to one another", and, because they treat the same subject in a different way and from a different angle, extend our understanding of it and bring us nearer to what is real and living. We know little about the truth except that it has many facets.

Part One contains poems about people, places and things, Part Two is mainly concerned with the narrative form.

Although we have put questions at the end of the book they are only suggestions—perhaps starters for thought and discussion. A good poet would not write a poem if what he wished to say could be expressed in prose. In consequence a good poem must always exceed a paraphrase. Yet there remains the problem of comprehension. Some teachers allow the poem to speak for itself while others cannot refrain from explaining every word and allusion. In the one case a pupil may be left without the gratification that comes with understanding; in the other his interest is likely to have been killed stone dead. Perhaps one of the best ways to understanding is by group discussion. If ten minutes of a lesson are spent in reading a poem (by teachers and others) and in coming to terms with words and syntax, followed by a longer period in directed discussion, then the poem is likely to be doing its job, growing into the life of the teacher and his pupils.

The poems in these books are arranged according to the needs of different age-groups. This does not mean that the poems in Book One can have no impact on that mythical creature "the adult". There is no final division between work which appeals to the pupil and work which appeals to the teacher. We could even say that if the teacher is bored by a poem he presents then it also bores his class.

Some of the poems may at first reading seem difficult. This is quite deliberate. Whether it is a matter of climbing a rock-face, solving a geometric problem or understanding a poem, there is a satisfaction in overcoming difficulties. Indeed what is called pleasure is often a by-product of such strenuous and directed effort.

Much poetry is about the inner life of man or the half hidden under- and over-tones of Nature. Just as you can't see your own face directly only through its reflection in a mirror, so you can't write about the world of inward experience directly only through counterparts and resemblances drawn from the external world. Shelley bodies forth his sense of the creative zest for life through the West Wind, Coleridge brings home to us abandonment and guilt by writing of a ship becalmed upon an oily sea. In *The Waste Land*, Eliot expresses modern man's longing for some spiritual refreshment and contact with a divine source of being by showing us people stumbling through a rocky desert and longing for rain. In the Gospels we have the pearl of great price, the man without a wedding garment, the many mansions of the divine city. These are poetic images. Through discussion and examples the pupil can be brought to understand the significance of such images and why certain inward experiences can be communicated in no other way.

The choral speaking of poetry enables a class to discover a poem's rhythm and drama by personal activity and by working as a team to blend their voices into one. It also enables pupils who have difficulties in speaking or reading aloud to gain confidence through the support of a group. For choral purposes a class can work as a unit, like a choir —soloists to the fore, the other members arranged on either side and behind. Rising volume and drama is gained by increasing the number of voices, line by line, for instance, until the whole class is employed; a falling volume by abstracting speaker by speaker. There are many possibilities and, once a class has acquired some experience of this activity, it should not be long before it is able to make an enterprising contribution to the arrangement.

In earlier times school children were often forced to learn yard lengths of arid verse. No good came of it unless one thinks of poetry as a disease against which they should be inoculated. However, many young people do enjoy and benefit from learning poetry—especially when it is poetry of their own choice. Scansion seems to us of no educational value in so far as it consists of putting lines of poetry into little stressed compartments which rarely fit English verse. But the learning of good poetry is a way of incorporating as part of oneself the rhythms, rhymes and images of English verse. Poetry is the expression of the thought and feeling of people who have thought and felt deeply about the human situation and expressed their discoveries with fluency and power. There cannot but be virtue in learning their poems by heart—but the operative word is "by heart".

Part 1

✻ Tonight at Noon*
(*for Charles Mingus and the Clayton Squares*)

Tonight at noon
Supermarkets will advertise 3d EXTRA on everything
Tonight at noon
Children from happy families will be sent to live in
    a home
Elephants will tell each other human jokes
America will declare peace on Russia
World War I generals will sell poppies in the
    streets on November 11th
The first daffodils of autumn will appear
When the leaves fall upwards to the trees

Tonight at noon
Pigeons will hunt cats through city backyards
Hitler will tell us to fight on the beaches and on the
    landing fields
A tunnel full of water will be built under Liverpool
Pigs will be sighted flying in formation over Woolton
and Nelson will not only get his eye back but his
    arm as well
White Americans will demonstrate for equal rights
in front of the Black House
and the Monster has just created Dr Frankenstein

* The title for this poem is taken from an L.P. by Charles Mingus "Tonight at Noon". Atlantic 1416.

Girls in bikinis are moonbathing
Folksongs are being sung by real folk
Artgalleries are closed to people over 21
Poets get their poems in the Top 20
Politicians are elected to insane asylums
There's jobs for everyone and nobody wants them
In back alleys everywhere teenage lovers are kissing
in broad daylight
In forgotten graveyards everywhere the dead will
    quietly
bury the living
and
You will tell me you love me
Tonight at noon

Adrian Henri

Mother the Wardrobe is Full of Infantrymen

mother the wardrobe is full of infantrymen
i did i asked them
but they snarled saying it was a mans life

mother there is a centurion tank in the parlour
i did i asked the officer
but he laughed saying 'Queens regulations'
(piano was out of tune anyway)

mother polish your identity bracelet
there is a mushroom cloud in the backgarden
i did i tried to bring in the cat
but it simply came to pieces in my hand
i did i tried to whitewash the windows

2

but there weren't any
i did i tried to hide under the stairs
but i couldn't get in for civil defence leaders
i did i tried ringing candid camera
but they crossed their hearts

i went for a policeman but they were looting the town
i went out for a fire engine but they were all upside
    down
i went for a priest but they were all on their knees
mother don't just lie there say something please
mother don't just lie there say something please

Roger McGough

The Honourable Company

He said, "It was our custom at the time
To join the Honourable Company of Straight
    Shooters.
Finding myself in the firing squad,
I naturally aimed straight.

Among the prisoners who would reserve
Their final diatribes for these occasions,
Was a young man questioning our values
Convicted for treason.

He paid the normal price, and cleaning our rifles
We turned our thoughts to what the peace might
    bring;
Of course there were many young men then
Questioning our values.

It is not his innocence that still disturbs me,
Nor his gesticulation and manner. It is
That having been young myself,
I recall no subversion.

On my part. As I have said, it was our custom
To join the Honourable Company of Straight
  Shooters.
Finding myself in the firing squad,
I naturally aimed straight."

Peter Champkin

✲ Auguries of Innocence

To see a World in a grain of sand,
And a Heaven in a wild flower,
Hold Infinity in the palm of your hand,
And Eternity in an hour.

A Robin redbreast in a cage
Puts all Heaven in a rage.
A dove-house fill'd with doves and pigeons
Shudders Hell thro' all its regions.
A dog starv'd at his master's gate
Predicts the ruin of the State.
A horse misus'd upon the road
Calls to Heaven for human blood.
Each outcry of the hunted hare
A fibre from the brain doth tear.
A skylark wounded in the wing,
A cherubim does cease to sing.
A game-cock clipt and arm'd for fight
Does the rising sun affright.
Every wolf's and lion's howl
Raises from Hell a Human soul.

4

The wild deer, wandering here and there,
Keeps the Human soul from care.
The lamb misus'd breeds public strife,
And yet forgives the butcher's knife.
The bat that flits at close of eve
Has left the brain that won't believe.
The owl that calls upon the night
Speaks the unbeliever's fright.

William Blake

Take one home for the Kiddies

On shallow straw, in shadeless glass,
Huddled by empty bowls they sleep:
No dark, no dam, no earth, no grass—
"Mam, get us one of them to keep."

Living toys are something novel,
But it soon wears off somehow.
Fetch the shoebox, fetch the shovel—
"Mam, we're playing funerals now."

Philip Larkin

Travelling Through the Dark

Travelling through the dark I found a deer
dead on the edge of the Wilson River road.
It is usually best to roll them into the canyon:
that road is narrow; to swerve might make more
    dead.

5

By glow of the tail-light I stumbled back of the car
and stood by the heap, a doe, a recent killing;
she had stiffened already, almost cold.
I dragged her off; she was large in the belly.

My fingers touching her side brought me the
    reason—
her side was warm; her fawn lay there waiting,
alive, still, never to be born.
Beside that mountain road I hesitated.

The car aimed ahead its lowered parking lights;
under the hood purred the steady engine.
I stood in the glare of the warm exhaust turning red;
around our group I could hear the wilderness listen.

I thought hard for us all—my only swerving—
then pushed her over the edge into the river.

William Stafford

Birds

Whatever the bird is, is perfect in the bird.
Weapon kestrel hard as a blade's curve,
thrush round as a mother or a full drop of water,
fruit-green parrot wise in his shrieking swerve—
all are what bird is and do not reach beyond bird.

Whatever the bird does is right for the bird to do—
cruel kestrel dividing in his hunger the sky,
thrush in the trembling dew beginning to sing,
parrot clinging and quarrelling and veiling his queer
    eye—
all these are as birds are and good for birds to do.

But I am torn and beleaguered by my own people.
The blood that feeds my heart is the blood they gave
me,
and my heart is the house where they gather and
fight for domination—
all different, all with a wish and a will to save me,
to turn me into the ways of other people.

If I could leave their battleground for the forest of a
bird
I could melt the past, the present and the future in
one
and find the words that lie behind all these
languages.
Then I could fuse my passions into one clear stone
and be simple to myself as the bird is to the bird.

Judith Wright

❋ A Dream of Horses

We were born grooms, in stable-straw we sleep still,
All our wealth horse-dung and the combings of
horses,
And all we can talk about is what horses ail.

Out of the night that gulfed beyond the palace-gate
There shook hooves and hooves and hooves of horses:
Our horses battered their stalls; their eyes jerked
white.

And we ran out, mice in our pockets, straw in our
hair,
Into darkness that was avalanching to horses
And a quake of hooves. Our lantern's little orange
flare

7

Made a round mask of our each sleep-dazed face,
Bodiless, or else bodied by horses
That whinnied and bit and cannoned the world
    from its place.

The tall palace was so white, the moon was so round,
Everything else this plunging of horses
To the rim of our eyes that strove for the shapes of
    the sound.

We crouched at our lantern, our bodies drank the
    din,
And we longed for a death trampled by such horses
As every grain of the earth had hooves and mane.

We must have fallen like drunkards into a dream
Of listening, lulled by the thunder of the horses:
We awoke, stiff: broad day had come.

Out through the gate the unprinted desert stretched
To stone and scorpion; our stable-horses
Lay in their straw, in a hag-sweat, listless and
    wretched.

Now let us, tied, be quartered by these poor horses,
If but doomsday's flames be great horses,
The for ever itself a circling of the hooves of horses.

Ted Hughes

The Horses

Barely a twelvemonth after
The seven days war that put the world to sleep,
Late in the evening the strange horses came.
By then we had made our covenant with silence,
But in the first few days it was so still
We listened to our breathing and were afraid.
On the second day
The radios failed; we turned the knobs; no answer.
On the third day a warship passed us, heading
    north,
Dead bodies piled on the deck. On the sixth day
A plane plunged over us into the sea. Thereafter
Nothing. The radios dumb;
And still they stand in corners of our kitchens,
And stand, perhaps, turned on, in a million rooms
All over the world. But now if they should speak,
If on a sudden they should speak again,
If on the stroke of noon a voice should speak,
We would not listen, we would not let it bring
That old bad world that swallowed its children
    quick
At one great gulp. We would not have it again.
Sometimes we think of the nations lying asleep,
Curled blindly in impenetrable sorrow,
And then the thought confounds us with its
    strangeness.
The tractors lie about our fields; at evening
They look like dank sea-monsters couched and
    waiting.
We leave them where they are and let them rust:
'They'll moulder away and be like other loam.'
We make our oxen drag our rusty ploughs,
Long laid aside. We have gone back
Far past our fathers' land.

                              And then, that evening
Late in the summer the strange horses came.
We heard a distant tapping on the road,
A deepening drumming; it stopped, went on again
And at the corner changed to hollow thunder.
We saw the heads
Like a wild wave charging and were afraid.
We had sold our horses in our fathers' time
To buy new tractors. Now they were strange to us
As fabulous steeds set on an ancient shield
Or illustrations in a book of knights.
We did not dare go near them. Yet they waited,
Stubborn and shy, as if they had been sent
By an old command to find our whereabouts
And that long-lost archaic companionship.
In the first moment we had never a thought
That they were creatures to be owned and used.
Among them were some half-a-dozen colts
Dropped in some wilderness of the broken world,
Yet new as if they had come from their own Eden.
Since then they have pulled our ploughs and borne
    our loads,
But that free servitude still can pierce our hearts.
Our life is changed; their coming our beginning.

Edwin Muir

❋ The Man in the Bowler Hat

I am the unnoticed, the unnoticeable man:
The man who sat on your right in the morning train:
The man you looked through like a windowpane:
The man who was the colour of the carriage, the
    colour of the mounting
Morning pipe smoke.

I am the man too busy with living to live,
Too hurried and worried to see and smell and touch:
The man who is patient too long and obeys too much
And wishes too softly and seldom.

I am the man they call the nation's backbone,
Who am boneless—playable catgut, pliable clay:
The Man they label Little lest one day
I dare to grow.

I am the rails on which the moment passes,
The megaphone for many words and voices:
I am graph, diagram,
Composite face.

I am the led, the easily-fed,
The tool, the not-quite-fool,
The would-be-safe-and-sound,
The uncomplaining bound,
The dust fine-ground,
Stone-for-a-statue waveworn pebble-round.

                                        A. S. J. Tessimond

The Unknown Citizen
(To JS/07/M/378)
(*This Marble Monument Is Erected by the State*)

He was found by the Bureau of Statistics to be
One against whom there was no official complaint,
And all the reports on his conduct agree
That, in the modern sense of an old-fashioned word,
    he was a saint,
For in everything he did he served the Greater
    Community.
Except for the War till the day he retired
He worked in a factory and never got fired,

But satisfied his employers, Fudge Motors Inc.
Yet he wasn't a scab or odd in his views,
For his Union reports that he paid his dues,
(Our report on his Union shows it was sound)
And our Social Psychology workers found
That he was popular with his mates and liked a
   drink.
The Press are convinced that he bought a paper
   every day
And that his reactions to advertisements were
   normal in every way.
Policies taken out in his name prove that he was
   fully insured,
And his Health-card shows he was once in hospital
   but left it cured.
Both Producers Research and High-Grade Living
   declare
He was fully sensible to the advantages of the
   Instalment Plan
And had everything necessary to the Modern Man,
A phonograph, a radio, a car and a frigidaire.
Our researchers into Public Opinion are content
That he held the proper opinions for the time of
   year.
When there was peace, he was for peace; when there
   was war, he went.
He was married and added five children to the
   population,
Which our Eugenist says was the right number for a
   parent of his generation,
And our teachers report that he never interfered
   with their education.
Was he free? Was he happy? The question is absurd:
Had anything been wrong, we should certainly have
   heard.

W. H. Auden

Jingle for Children

I am a poor man in a train,
I go to work and come again
And there is nothing in my brain
But go to work and come again.

I am a person in a crowd,
I cannot speak my thoughts aloud.
To the distinguished and the proud
I cannot speak my thoughts aloud.

I am a leader and my power
Can kill your leaders in an hour.
I am a poor man in a train,
I go to work and come again.

I am a person in a crowd,
I cannot speak my thoughts aloud.

Peter Champkin

❋ Lollocks

By sloth on sorrow fathered,
These dusty-featured Lollocks
Have their nativity in all disordered
Backs of cupboard drawers.

They play hide and seek
Among collars and novels
And empty medicine bottles,
And letters from abroad
That never will be answered.

Every sultry night
They plague little children,
Gurgling from the cistern,
Humming from the air,
Skewing up the bed-clothes,
Twitching the blind.

When the imbecile agèd
Are over-long in dying
And the nurse drowses,
Lollocks come skipping
Up the tattered stairs
And are nasty together
In the bed's shadow.

The signs of their presence
Are boils on the neck,
Dreams of vexation suddenly recalled
In the middle of the morning,
Languor after food.

Men cannot see them
Men cannot hear them,
Do not believe in them—
But suffer the more,
Both in neck and belly.

Women can see them—
O those naughty wives
Who sit by the fireside
Munching bread and honey,
Watching them in mischief
From corners of their eyes,
Slily allowing them to lick
Honey-sticky fingers.

Sovereign against Lollocks,
Are hard broom and soft broom,
To well comb the hair,
To well brush the shoe,
And to pay every debt
So soon as it's due.

Robert Graves

In Praise of Herbs

And can the physician make sick men well,
And can the magician a fortune divine,
Without lily, germander and sops in wine,
And sweet briar,
And bonfire,
And strawberry wire,
And columbine?

With in-and-out, in-and-out, round as a ball
With hither and thither as straight as a line,
With lily, germander and sops in wine,
And sweet briar,
And bonfire,
And strawberry wire,
And columbine.

When Saturn did live, there lived no poor,
The king and the beggar on roots did dine,
With lily, germander, and sops in wine,
And sweet briar,
And bonfire,
And strawberry wire,
And columbine.

Anonymous

Charms

Against the evil spirit
In the morning when ye rise,
Wash your hands, and cleanse your eyes,
Next be sure ye have a care,
To disperse the water farre.
For as farre as that doth light,
So farre keepes the evill Spright.

Against witches
Bring the holy crust of Bread,
Lay it underneath the head;
'Tis a certain Charm to keep
Hags away, while Children sleep.

Against fears at night
If ye feare to be affrighted
When ye are (by chance) benighted:
In your pocket for a trust,
Carrie nothing but a Crust:
For that holy piece of Bread
Charmes the danger, and the dread.

Against love
If so be a Toad be laid
In a sheeps-skin newly flaid,
And that ty'd to man, 'twil sever
Him and his affections ever.

Robert Herrick

Spate in Winter Midnight

The streams fall down and through the darkness bear
Such wild and shaking hair,
Such looks beyond a cool surmise,
Such lamentable uproar from night skies
As turns the owl from honey of blood and make
Great stags stand still to hear the darkness shake.

Through Troys of bracken and Babel towers of rocks
Shrinks now the looting fox,
Fearful to touch the thudding ground
And flattened to it by the mastering sound.
And roebuck stilt and leap sideways; their skin
Twitches like water on the fear within.

Black hills are slashed white with this falling grace
Whose violence buckles space
To a sheet-iron thunder. This
Is noise made universe, whose still centre is
Where the cold adder sleeps in his small bed,
Curled neatly round his neat and evil head.

Norman MacCaig

Inversnaid

This darksome burn, horseback brown,
His rollrock highroad roaring down,
In coop and in comb the fleece of his foam
Flutes and low to the lake falls home.

A windpuff-bonnet of fawn-froth
Turns and twindles over the broth
Of a pool so pitchblack, fell-frowning,
It rounds and rounds Despair to drowning.

Degged with dew, dappled with dew
Are the groins of the braes that the brook treads
    through,
Wiry heathpacks, flitches of fern,
And the beadbonny ash that sits over the burn.

What would the world be, once bereft
Of wet and of wildness? Let them be left,
O let them be left, wildness and wet;
Long live the weeds and the wilderness yet.

Gerard Manley Hopkins

Ode to the West Wind

I

O wild West Wind, thou breath of Autumn's being,
    Thou from whose unseen presence the leaves dead
Are driven, like ghosts from an enchanter fleeing.

    Yellow, and black, and pale, and hectic red,
Pestilence-stricken multitudes: O thou
    Who chariotest to their dark wintry bed

The wingèd seeds, where they lie cold and low,
    Each like a corpse within its grave, until
Thine azure sister of the Spring shall blow

    Her clarion o'er the dreaming earth, and fill
(Driving sweet buds like flocks to feed in air)
    With living hues and odours plain and hill:

Wild Spirit, which art moving everywhere;
Destroyer and preserver: hear, O hear!

Thou on whose stream, 'mid the steep sky's
    commotion,
  Loose clouds like earth's decaying leaves are shed,
Shook from the tangled boughs of heaven and ocean,

  Angels of rain and lightning: there are spread
On the blue surface of thine aëry surge,
  Like the bright hair uplifted from the head

Of some fierce Maenad, even from the dim verge
  Of the horizon to the zenith's height,
The locks of the approaching storm. Thou dirge

  Of the dying year, to which this closing night
Will be the dome of a vast sepulchre,
  Vaulted with all thy congregated might

Of vapours, from whose solid atmosphere
Black rain, and fire, and hail will burst: O hear!

III

Thou who didst waken from his summer dreams
  The blue Mediterranean, where he lay
Lulled by the coil of his crystàlline streams,

  Beside a pumice isle in Baiæ's bay,
And saw in sleep old palaces and towers
  Quivering within the wave's intenser day.

All overgrown with azure moss, and flowers,
  So sweet, the sense faints picturing them! Thou
For whose path the Atlantic's level powers

Cleave themselves into chasms, while far below
The sea-blooms and the oozy woods which wear
  The sapless foliage of the ocean, know

Thy voice, and suddenly grow gray with fear,
And tremble, and despoil themselves: O hear!

IV

If I were a dead leaf thou mightest bear;
  If I were a swift cloud to fly with thee;
A wave to pant beneath thy power, and share

  The impulse of thy strength, only less free
Than thou, O uncontrollable! if even
  I were as in my boyhood, and could be

The comrade of thy wanderings over heaven,
  As then, when to outstrip thy skiey speed
Scarce seemed a vision—I would ne'er have striven

  As thus with thee in prayer in my sore need.
O lift me as a wave, a leaf, a cloud!
  I fall upon the thorns of life! I bleed!

A heavy weight of hours has chained and bowed
One too like thee—tameless, and swift, and proud.

V

Make me thy lyre, even as the forest is:
  What if my leaves are falling like its own!
The tumult of thy mighty harmonies

  Will take from both a deep autumnal tone,
Sweet though in sadness. Be thou, Spirit fierce,
  My spirit! Be thou me, impetuous one!

Drive my dead thoughts over the universe
   Like withered leaves to quicken a new birth;
And, by the incantation of this verse,

   Scatter, as from an unextinguished hearth
Ashes and sparks, my words among mankind!
   Be through my lips to unawakened earth

The trumpet of a prophecy! O Wind,
If Winter comes, can Spring be far behind?

Percy Bysshe Shelley

❋ On the Balcony

In front of the sombre mountains, a faint, lost ribbon
   of rainbow;
And between us and it, the thunder;
And down below in the green wheat, the labourers
Stand like dark stumps, still in the green wheat.

You are near to me, and your naked feet in their
   sandals,
And through the scent of the balcony's naked timber
I distinguish the scent of your hair: so now the
   limber
Lightning falls from heaven.

Adown the pale-green glacier river floats
A dark boat through the gloom—and whither?
The thunder roars. But still we have each other!
The naked lightnings in the heavens dither
And disappear—what have we but each other?
The boat has gone.

D. H. Lawrence

I know where I'm going

I know where I'm going,
I know who's going with me,
I know who I love,
But the dear knows who I'll marry.

I'll have stockings of silk
Shoes of fine green leather,
Combs to buckle my hair
And a ring for every finger.

Feather beds are soft,
Painted rooms are bonny;
But I'd leave them all
To go with my love Johnny.

Some say he's dark,
I say he's bonny,
He's the flower of them all
My handsome, winsome Johnny.

I know where I'm going,
I know who's going with me,
I know who I love,
But the dear knows who I'll marry.

Anonymous

To his Love

Shall I compare thee to a summer's day?
    Thou art more lovely and more temperate:
Rough winds so shake the darling buds of May,
    And summer's lease hath all too short a date:

Sometime too hot for the eye of heaven shines,
    And often is his gold complexion dimm'd:
And every fair from fair sometime declines,
    By chance, or nature's changing course, untrimm'd.

But thy eternal summer shall not fade
    Nor lose possession of that fair thou owest;
Nor shall death brag thou wanderest in his shade,
    When in eternal lines to time thou growest:

So long as men can breathe, or eyes can see,
So long lives this, and this gives life to thee.

William Shakespeare

✤ Eternity

He who binds to himself a joy
Doth the winged life destroy,
But he who kisseth a joy as it flies
Lives in Eternity's sunrise.

William Blake

If I were the Earth

If I were the earth
And you a tree,
I'd feel you growing
Out of me.

If you were a bird
And I the air,
You'd not escape me
Anywhere.

If you were a stone
I, a river in flood,
Surely should feel you
Through my blood.

The stone has pierced me
The bird has died,
The tree will uphold me
Crucified.

Anonymous

O, My Luve is Like a Red, Red Rose

O, my luve is like a red, red rose,
    That's newly sprung in June:
O, my luve is like the melodie
    That's sweetly played in tune.

As fair art thou, my bonnie lass,
    So deep in luve am I;
And I will luve thee still, my dear,
    Till a' the seas gang dry.

Till a' the seas gang dry, my dear,
    And the rocks melt wi' the sun:
And I will luve thee still, my dear,
    While the sands o' life shall run.

And fare thee weel, my only luve,
    And fare thee weel a while!
And I will come again, my luve,
    Tho' it were ten thousand mile!

Robert Burns

The Sick Rose

O rose thou art sick:
The invisible worm
That flies in the night
In the howling storm,

Has found out thy bed
Of crimson joy,
And his dark secret love
Does thy life destroy.

William Blake

As I walked out one Evening

As I walked out one evening,
Walking down Bristol Street,
The crowds upon the pavement
Were fields of harvest wheat.

And down by the brimming river
I heard a lover sing
Under an arch of the railway:
'Love has no ending.

'I'll love you, dear, I'll love you
Till China and Africa meet
And the river jumps over the mountain
And the salmon sing in the street.

'I'll love you till the ocean
Is folded and hung up to dry
And the seven stars go squawking
Like geese about the sky.

'The years shall run like rabbits
For in my arms I hold
The Flower of the Ages
And the first love of the world.'

But all the clocks in the city
Began to whirr and chime:
'O let not Time deceive you,
You cannot conquer Time.

'In the burrows of the Nightmare
Where Justice naked is,
Time watches from the shadow
And coughs when you would kiss.

'In headaches and in worry
Vaguely life leaks away,
And Time will have his fancy
To-morrow or to-day.

'Into many a green valley
Drifts the appalling snow;
Time breaks the threaded dances
And the diver's brilliant bow.

'O plunge your hands in water,
Plunge them in up to the wrist;
Stare, stare in the basin
And wonder what you've missed.

'The glacier knocks in the cupboard,
The desert sighs in the bed,
And the crack in the tea-cup opens
A lane to the land of the dead.

'Where the beggars raffle the banknotes
And the Giant is enchanting to Jack,
And the Lily-white Boy is a Roarer
And Jill goes down on her back.

'O look, look in the mirror,
O look in your distress;
Life remains a blessing
Although you cannot bless.

'O stand, stand at the window
As the tears scald and start;
You shall love your crooked neighbour
With your crooked heart.'

It was late, late in the evening,
The lovers they were gone;
The clocks had ceased their chiming
And the deep river ran on.

W. H. Auden

※ Western Wind

O Western wind, when wilt thou blow,
That the small rain down can rain?
Christ, If my love were in my arms,
And I in my bed again!

Anonymous

White Clouds

White clouds are in the sky,
Great shoulders of the hills
Between us two must lie.
The road is rough and far.
Deep fords between us are.
I pray you not to die.

Anonymous
A Chinese Poem (about 1121 B.C.)

Li Fu-jen

The sound of her silk skirt has stopped.
On the marble pavement dust grows.
Her empty room is cold and still.
Fallen leaves are piled against the doors.
   Longing for that lovely lady
How can I bring my aching heart to rest?

The above poem was written by Wu-ti when his
mistress, Li Fu-jen, died. Unable to bear his grief,
he sent for wizards from all parts of China, hoping
that they would be able to put him into communi-
cation with her spirit. At last one of them managed to
project her shape on to a curtain. The emperor cried:

Is it, or isn't it?
I stand and look
The swish, swish of a silk skirt.
How slow she comes!

translated by Arthur Waley

Break, Break, Break

Break, break, break,
　　On thy cold grey stones, O Sea!
And I would that my tongue could utter
　　The thoughts that arise in me.

O well for the fisherman's boy,
　　That he shouts with his sister at play!
O well for the sailor lad,
　　That he sings in his boat on the bay!

And the stately ships go on
　　To their haven under the hill;
But O for the touch of a vanish'd hand,
　　And the sound of a voice that is still!

Break, break, break,
　　At the foot of thy crags, O Sea!
But the tender grace of a day that is dead
　　Will never come back to me.

Alfred, Lord Tennyson

✤ # A Poison Tree

I was angry with my friend:
I told my wrath, my wrath did end.
I was angry with my foe:
I told it not, my wrath did grow.

And I water'd it in fears,
Night and morning with my tears;
And I sunned it with smiles,
And with soft deceitful wiles.

And it grew both day and night,
Till it bore an apple bright;
And my foe beheld it shine,
And he knew that it was mine,

And into my garden stole
When the night had veil'd the pole:
In the morning glad I see
My foe outstretch'd beneath the tree.

William Blake

A Case of Murder

They should not have left him there alone,
Alone that is except for the cat.
He was only nine, not old enough
To be left alone in a basement flat,
Alone, that is, except for the cat.
A dog would have been a different thing,
A big gruff dog with slashing jaws,
But a cat with round eyes mad as gold,
Plump as a cushion with tucked-in paws—
Better have left him with a fair-sized rat!
But what they did was leave him with a cat.
He hated that cat; he watched it sit,
A buzzing machine of soft black stuff,
He sat and watched and he hated it,
Snug in its fur, hot blood in a muff,
And its mad gold stare and the way it sat
Crooning dark warmth: he loathed all that.
So he took Daddy's stick and he hit the cat.
Then quick as a sudden crack in glass
It hissed, black flash, to hiding place
In the dust and dark beneath the couch,
And he followed the grin on his new-made face,

A wide-eyed, frightened snarl of a grin,
And he took the stick and he thrust it in,
Hard and quick in the furry dark.
The black fur squealed and he felt his skin
Prickle with sparks of dry delight.
Then the cat again came into sight,
Shot for the door that wasn't quite shut,
But the boy, quick too, slammed fast the door:
The cat, half-through, was cracked like a nut
And the soft black thud was dumped on the floor.
Then the boy was suddenly terrified
And he bit his knuckles and cried and cried;
But he had to do something with the dead thing
    there.
His eyes squeezed beads of salty prayer
But the wound of fear gaped wide and raw;
He dared not touch the thing with his hands
So he fetched a spade and shovelled it
And dumped the load of heavy fur
In the spidery cupboard under the stair
Where it's been for years, and though it died
It's grown in that cupboard and its hot low purr
Grows slowly louder year by year:
There'll not be a corner for the boy to hide
When the cupboard swells and all sides split
And the huge black cat pads out of it.

Vernon Scannell

Spain, 1809

All day we had ridden through scarred, tawny hills.
At last the cool
Of splashing water. Then two blackened mills,
A slaughtered mule.

And there, crag-perched, the village—San Pedro—
We came to burn.
(Two convoys ambushed in the gorge below.
They had to learn.)

Not a sound. Not a soul. Not a goat left behind.
They had been wise.
Those death's-head hovels watched us, bleared and
    blind,
With holes for eyes.

Down the one street's foul gutter slowly crawled
Like blood, dark-red,
The wine from goatskins, slashed and hacked, that
    sprawled
Like human dead.

From a black heap, like some charred funeral-pyre,
Curled up, forlorn,
Grey wisps of smoke, where they had fed the fire
With their last corn.

What hatred in that stillness! Suddenly
An infant's cry.
Child, mother, bedrid crone—we found the three,
Too frail to fly.

We searched their very straw—one wineskin there.
We grinned with thirst,
And yet?—that Spanish hate!—what man would dare
To taste it first?

Below, our Captain called, 'Bring down the wench'.
We brought her down—
Dark brooding eyes that faced the smiling French
With sullen frown.

'Senora, we are sent to burn the place,
Your house I spare.'
Her proud chin nestled on her baby's face,
Still silent there.

'Cold cheer you leave us!—one poor skin of wine!
Before we sup,
You will honour us, Senora?' At his sign
One filled a cup.

Calmly she took and, drinking, coldly smiled;
We breathed more free.
But grimly our captain watched her—'Now your
    child.'
Impassively,

She made the small mouth swallow. All was well.
The street was fired.
And we, by that brave blaze, as twilight fell,
Sat gaily tired,

Laughing and eating, while the wine went round,
Carefree, until
A child's scream through the darkness. At the sound
Our hearts stood still.

Dumbly we glanced in one another's eyes.
Our thirst was dead.
And in its place once more that grim surmise
Upreared its head.

One dragged her to the firelight. Ashen-grey,
She hissed—'I knew
Not even the straw where an old woman lay
Was safe from you.

'Now you are paid!' I never loved their wine,
Had tasted none.
I will not tell, under that white moonshine,
What things were done.

Twenty men mad with drink, and rage, and dread,
Frenzied with pain—
That night the quiet millstream dribbled red
With blood of Spain.

Under the moon across the gaunt sierra
I fled alone.
Their balls whizzed wide. But in each tree lurked
    terror,
In each stone.

Yes, men are brave. (Earth were a happier place,
Were men less so.)
But I remember one pale woman's face
In San Pedro.

F. L. Lucas

They that have Power to Hurt

They that have power to hurt, and will do none,
    That do not do the thing they most do show,
Who, moving others, are themselves as stone,
    Unmovèd, cold, and to temptation slow,—

They rightly do inherit Heaven's graces,
    And husband nature's riches from expense;
They are the lords and owners of their faces,
    Others, but stewards of their excellence.

The summer's flower is to the summer sweet,
  Though to itself it only live and die;
But if that flower with base infection meet,
  The basest weed outbraves his dignity:

For sweetest things turn sourest by their deeds;
Lilies that fester smell far worse than weeds.

William Shakespeare

Nationality

I have grown past hate and bitterness,
I see the world as one;
Yet, though I can no longer hate,
My son is still my son,
All men at God's round table sit,
And all men must be fed;
But this loaf in my hand,
This loaf is my son's bread.

Mary Gilmore

❊ Lucifer in Starlight

On a starred night Prince Lucifer uprose.
Tired of his dark dominion swung the fiend
  Above the rolling ball in cloud part screened,
Where sinners hugged their spectre of repose.
Poor prey to his hot fit of pride were those.
  And now upon his western wing he leaned,
  Now his huge bulk o'er Afric's sands careened,
Now the black planet shadowed Arctic snows.

Soaring through wider zones that pricked his scars
   With memory of the old revolt from Awe,
He reached a middle height, and at the stars,
Which are the brain of heaven, he looked, and sank.
Around the ancient track marched, rank on rank,
   The army of unalterable law.

George Meredith

Innocent's Song

Who's that knocking on the window,
Who's that standing at the door,
What are all those presents
Lying on the kitchen floor?

Who is the smiling stranger
With hair as white as gin,
What is he doing with the children
And who could have let him in?

Why has he rubies on his fingers,
A cold, cold crown on his head,
Why, when he caws his carol,
Does the salty snow run red?

Why does he ferry my fireside
As a spider on a thread,
His fingers made of fuses
And his tongue of gingerbread.

Why does the world before him
Melt in a million suns?
Why do his yellow, yearning eyes
Burn like saffron buns?

Watch where he comes walking
Out of the Christmas Flame,
Dancing, double talking:

Herod is his name.

Charles Causley

❋ Schoolmaster

The window gives onto the white trees,
The master looks out of it at the trees,
for a long time, he looks for a long time
out through the window at the trees,
breaking his chalk slowly in one hand.
And it's only the rules of long division.
And he's forgotten the rules of long division.
Imagine not remembering long division!
A mistake on the blackboard, a mistake.
We watch him with a different attention
needing no one to hint to us about it,
there's more than difference in this attention.
The schoolmaster's wife has gone away,
we do not know where she has gone to,
we do not know why she has gone,
what we know is his wife has gone away.

His clothes are neither new nor in the fashion;
wearing the suit which he always wears
and which is neither new nor in the fashion
the master goes downstairs to the cloakroom.
He fumbles in his pocket for a ticket.
'What's the matter? Where is that ticket?
Perhaps I never picked up my ticket.
Where is the thing?' Rubbing his forehead.

'Oh, here it is. I'm getting old.
Don't argue auntie dear, I'm getting old.
You can't do much about getting old.'
We hear the door below creaking behind him.

The window gives onto the white trees.
The trees there are high and wonderful,
but they are not why we are looking out.
We look in silence at the schoolmaster.
He has a bent back and clumsy walk,
He moves without defences, clumsily,
worn out I ought to have said, clumsily.
Snow falling on him softly through the silence
turns him to white under the white trees.
He whitens into white like the trees.
A little longer will make him so white
we shall not see him in the whitened trees.

Yevgeny Yevtushenko
translated by Robin Milner-
Gulland and Peter Levi, S.J.

The French Master

Everyone in class two at the Grammar School
had heard of Walter Bird, known as Wazo.
They said he'd behead each dullard and fool
or, instead, carve off a tail for fun.

Wazo's cane buzzed like a bee in the air.
Quietly, quietly, in the desks of Form III
sneaky Wazo tweaked our ears and our hair.
Walter Wazo, public enemy No. 1.

Five feet tall, he married sweet Doreen Wall
and combmarks his vaselined hair;
his hands still fluttering ridiculously small,
His eyes the colour of a poison bottle.

Who'd think he'd falter poor love-sick Walter
As bored he read out Lettres de Mon Moulin;
His mouth had begun to soften and alter,
And Class IV ribbed him as only boys can.

Perhaps through kissing his wife to a moan
had alone changed the shape of his lips,
till the habit of her mouth became his own;
No more Walter Wazo, Public Enemy No. 1.

"Boy" he'd whine, "yes, please decline the verb to
    hate,"
In tones dulcet and mild as a girl's,
"Sorry Sir, can't Sir, must go to the lav,"
Whilst Wazo stared out of this world.

Till one day in May Wazo buzzed like a bee,
And stung twice many a warm, inky hand;
he stormed through the form, a catastrophe
returned to this world, No. 1.

Alas, alas, to the VIth Form's disgrace
nobody could quote Villon to that villain.
Again the nasty old mouth zipped on his face,
And not a weak-bladdered boy in the class.

Was Doreen being kissed by a Mr Anon?
Years later I purred, "Your dear wife, Mr Bird?"
Teeth bared, how he glared before stamping on;
And suddenly I felt sorry for the bastard.

                                    Dannie Abse

✤ Food for Powder

Prince Henry
   But tell me, Jack,
whose fellows are these that come after?
Sir John Falstaff
Mine, Hal, mine.
Prince Henry
I did never see such pitiful rascals.
Sir John Falstaff
Tut, tut; good enough to toss; food for powder, food
for powder; they'll fill a pit as well as better: tush,
man, mortal men, mortal men.

William Shakespeare
(Henry IV, Part I)

A Square Dance

In Flanders fields in Northern France
They're all doing a brand new dance
It makes you happy and out of breath
And it's called the Dance of Death

Everybody stands in line
Everybody's feeling fine
We're all going to a hop
1—2—3 and over the top

It's the dance designed to thrill
It's the mustard gas quadrille
A dance for men—girls have no say in it
For your partner is a bayonet

See how the dancers sway and run
To the rhythm of the gun
Swing your partner dos-y-doed
All around the shells explode

Honour your partner form a square
Smell the burning in the air
Over the barbed wire kicking high
Men like shirts hung out to dry

Everybody claps his hand
To the swinging German Band
When you're tired hold your head
Stumble, fall, pretend you're dead

When you're ready for some fun
Up you get and kill a hun
In khaki evening dress you're grand
The Victor Sylvester of no man's land

In Flanders fields where mortars blaze
They're all doing the latest craze
Khaki dancers out of breath
Doing the glorious Dance of Death
Doing the glorious (*clap, clap*) Dance of Death.

Roger McGough

Futility

Move him into the sun—
Gently its touch awoke him once,
At home, whispering of fields unsown.
Always it woke him, even in France,
Until this morning and this snow.
If anything might rouse him now
The kind old sun will know.

Think how it wakes the seeds,—
Woke, once, the clays of a cold star.
Are limbs, so dear-achieved, are sides,
Full-nerved—still warm—too hard to stir?
Was it for this the clay grew tall?
—O what made fatuous sunbeams toil
To break earth's sleep at all.

Wilfred Owen

Attack

At dawn the ridge emerges massed and dun
In the wild purple of the glow'ring sun,
Smouldering through spouts of drifting smoke that
     shroud
The menacing scarred slope; and, one by one,
Tanks creep and topple forward to the wire.
The barrage roars and lifts. Then, clumsily bowed
With bombs and guns and shovels and battle-gear,
Men jostle and climb to meet the bristling fire.
Lines of grey, muttering faces, masked with fear,
They leave their trenches, going over the top,
While time ticks blank and busy on their wrists,
And hope, with furtive eyes and grappling fists,
Flounders in mud. O Jesus, make it stop!

Siegfried Sassoon

The Chances

I mind as 'ow the night afore that show
Us five got talking,—we was in the know,—
"Over the top to-morrer; boys, we're for it,
First wave we are, first ruddy wave; that's tore it."

"Ah well," says Jimmy,—an' 'e's seen some
    scrappin'—
"There ain't more nor five things as can 'appen;—
Ye get knocked out; else wounded—bad or cushy;
Scuppered; or nowt except yer feeling mushy."

One of us got the knock-out, blown to chops.
T'other was hurt like, losing' both 'is props.
An' one, to use the word of 'ypocrites,
'Ad the misfortoon to be took be Fritz.
Now me, I wasn't scratched, praise God Almighty
(Though next time please I'll thank 'im for a blighty),
But poor young Jim, 'e's living' an' 'e's not;
'E reckoned 'e'd five chances, an' 'e 'ad;
'E's wounded, killed, and pris'ner, all the lot,
The bloody lot all rolled in one. Jim's mad.

Wilfred Owen

Grass

Pile the bodies high at Austerlitz and Waterloo.
Shovel them under and let me work—
    I am the grass; I cover all.

And pile them high at Gettysburg
And pile them high at Ypres and Verdun.
Shovel them under and let me work.
Two years, ten years, and passengers ask the
    conductor:
    What place is this?
    Where are we now?

    I am the grass.
    Let me work.

Carl Sandburg

43

My Raggamuffins

I've led my raggamuffins where they are peppered.
There's not three of my hundred and fifty left alive.
And they are for the town's end and to beg during life.
William Shakespeare
(Henry IV, Part I)

✤ War Poet

I am the man who looked for peace and found
My own eyes barbed.
I am the man who groped for words and found
An arrow in my hand.
I am the builder whose firm walls surround
A slipping land.
When I grow sick or mad
Mock me not nor chain me:
When I reach for the wind
Cast me not down:
Though my face is a burnt book
And a wasted town.

Sidney Keyes

Enfidaville

In the church, fallen like dancers
lie the virgin and St Thérèse
on little pillows of dust.
The detonations of the last few days
tore down the ornamental plasters.
Shivered the hands of Christ.

The men and women who moved like candles
in and out of the houses and the streets
are all gone. The white houses are bare
black cages; no one is left to greet
the ghosts tugging at doorhandles,
opening doors that are not there.

Now the daylight coming in from the fields
like a labourer, tired and sad
is peering among the wreckage, goes
past some corners as though with averted head
not looking at the pain this town holds,
seeing no one move behind the windows.

But they are coming back; they begin to search
like ants among their debris, finding in it
a bed or a piano and carrying it out.
Who would not love them at this minute?
I seem again to meet
The blue eyes of the images in the church.

Keith Douglas

Parachutists

Plummets from sky sway the beautiful dancers
Touching no land but the gold of the morning,
Opens behind them the blossoming silken
Bloom like a garland a delicate warning

Sliding and gliding like spirits from heaven
Slung from the stars, they draw patterns on silence,
With balance of ballet but swiftly as bullets
They pilot their plunge from the blue into Devon

Whirling from nowhere, to Africa, Russia,
Dancing through clouds to the wild heart of England.
Light as death's angels they march through the
    azure
Drifting through space like the earth's bright pollen

Stealers of beauty, they curl round the eagle
Wrestlers with lightning they open in crosses:
These are the bravest, who soar without equal
But never shall rival the heights of my wishes.

Beings less free than my hopes, they come falling,
Dwindling, proud dancers, to death and to danger,
For over the headlands the watchers are calling
And the king of the air is marked down as a stranger

And you are less free than my love for the people,
Those who are waiting, amazed at your coming,
The solid, the silent, the simple, the subtle.
Who are rooted in earth like my love and my longing.
                                        Francis Scarfe

❧ The Soldier Addresses his Body

I shall be mad if you get smashed about;
we've had good times together, you and I;
although you groused a bit when luck was out,
and a girl turned us down, or we went dry.

Yet there's a world of things we haven't done,
countries not seen, where people do strange things;
eat fish alive, and mimic in the sun
the solemn gestures of their stone-grey kings.

I've heard of forests that are dim at noon
where snakes and creepers wrestle all day long;
where vivid beasts grow pale with the full moon,
gibber and cry, and wail a mad old song;

because at the full moon the Hippogriff
with crinkled ivory snout and agate feet,
with his green eye will glare them cold and stiff
for the coward Wyvern to come down and eat.

Vodka and kvass, and bitter mountain wines
we've never drunk, nor snatched at bursting grapes
to pelt slim girls among Sicilian vines,
who'd flicker through the leaves, faint frolic shapes.

Yes, there are many things we have not done,
but it's a sweat to knock them into rhyme,
let's have a drink, and give the cards a run
and leave dull verse to the dull peaceful time.

Edgell Rickword

Roman Wall Blues

Over the heather the wet wind blows,
I've lice in my tunic and a cold in my nose.

The rain comes pattering out of the sky,
I'm a Wall soldier, I don't know why.

The mist creeps over the hard grey stone,
My girl's in Tungria; I sleep alone.

Aulus goes hanging around her place,
I don't like his manners, I don't like his face.

Piso's a Christian, he worships a fish;
There'd be no kissing if he had his wish.

She gave me a ring but I diced it away;
I want my girl and I want my pay.

When I'm a veteran with only one eye
I shall do nothing but look at the sky.

W. H. Auden

❊ Aikichi Kuboyama

"The world's first-known hydrogen bomb victim died
yesterday in a Tokyo hospital after an illness of six
months: Aikichi Kuboyama, a fisherman, on the boat
'Lucky Dragon'."

(From "Western Morning News",
September 24th, 1954)

Come closer. Watch the newly-born disease.
I am Aikichi Kuboyama, stranger.
Aikichi Kuboyama, Japanese:
Small boat. Strong fish. Yellow sea. Very danger.
Nose to the Wind. Seasalt. Seasharp. Seaspeck
Of mushroom cloud higher than Fuji. Heat.
I—fingers in the fishnets upon deck,
I—sick and yellow underneath the sheet,
Life squeezed into the smallness of a pill
Tasting of milk as when it first began,
Stillness for one that never would keep still,
Dream for a very dreaming kind of man
That worked for not too long and took to bed,
But in his time fished hard in stream and sea
And loved the fall of blossom on the head,
And blessed o-cha, the aromatic tea,

And owned too much in sea, too little in soil:
(Green mulberry, brown worm, kimono blue)
And lived on octopus thick-sliced and boiled
Octopus eyes that gaze inside of you.

Night. Torches. Cormorants in pitch-pine heat
Nagara river dances in the dusk
Slow softly swaying on tabi-clad feet.
Go, feed the holy horse on holy rusk.
Go, find the cormorants. O, find the place
Between the whirlpools. Find and tell me how
Downstream past Gifu (wind upon the face)
In water-lapping dactyls water splashes
Against the heart, against the tar-stained bow.
Aikichi Kuboyama dies of ashes.

Zofia Ilinska

Your Attention Please

The Polar DEW has just warned that
A nuclear rocket strike of
At least one thousand megatons
Has been launched by the enemy
Directly at our major cities.
This announcement will take
Two and a quarter minutes to make,
You therefore have a further
Eight and a quarter minutes
To comply with the shelter
Requirements published in the Civil
Defence Code—section Atomic Attack.

A specially shortened Mass
Will be broadcast at the end
Of this announcement—
Protestant and Jewish services
Will begin simultaneously—
Select your wavelength immediately
According to instructions
In the Defence Code. Do not
Take well-loved pets (including birds)
Into your shelter—they will consume
Fresh air. Leave the old and bed-
ridden, you can do nothing for them.
Remember to press the sealing
Switch when everyone is in
The shelter. Set the radiation
Aerial, turn on the geiger barometer.
Turn off your Television now.
Turn off your radio immediately
The Services end. At the same time
Secure explosion plugs in the ears
Of each member of your family. Take
Down your plasma flasks. Give your children
The pills marked one and two
In the C.D. green container, then put
Them to bed. Do not break
The inside airlock seals until
The radiation All Clear shows
(Watch for the cuckoo in your
perspex panel), or your District
Touring Doctor rings your bell.
If before this, your air becomes
Exhausted or if any of your family
Is critically injured, administer
The capsules marked 'Valley Forge'
(Red pocket in No. 1 Survival Kit)
For painless death. (Catholics

Will have been instructed by their priests
What to do in this eventuality.)
This announcement is ending. Our President
Has already given orders for
Massive retaliation—it will be
Decisive. Some of us may die.
Remember, statistically
It is not likely to be you.
All flags are flying fully dressed
On Government buildings—the sun is shining.
Death is the least we have to fear.
We are all in the hands of God,
Whatever happens happens by His Will,
Now go quickly to your shelters.

Peter Porter

Bombs

Shuddered, I did, to think of men,
Not unlike me, with Hydrogen
Oblivion at their trigger finger
And scant lucidity in anger;
Until I thought death is inbuilt
In you and me, though these cobalt
Contraptions—and of heavy water—
Make us think it's an alien matter.
In plural or in singular,
Dying of course, is what we are.

Where there is power there is abuse;
I touch my heart and touch the fuse
Of time (it everyday decreases
And soon will blow this world to pieces)
With something not unlike aplomb;
It's nice to think one has the Bomb!

Thomas Blackburn

The Convergence of the Twain

(*Lines on the loss of the "Titanic"*)

I

In a solitude of the sea
Deep from human vanity,
And the Pride of Life that planned her, stilly
    couches she.

II

Steel chambers, late the pyres
Of her salamandrine fires,
Cold currents thrid, and turn to rhythmic tidal lyres.

III

Over the mirrors meant
To glass the opulent
The sea-worm crawls—grotesque, slimed, dumb,
    indifferent.

IV

Jewels in joy designed
To ravish the sensuous mind
Lie lightless, all their sparkles bleared and black
    and blind.

V

Dim moon-eyed fishes near
Gaze at the gilded gear
And query: "What does this vain gloriousness
    down here?' . . .

VI

Well: while was fashioning
This creature of cleaving wing,
The Immanent Will that stirs and urges everything

VII

Prepared a sinister mate
For her—so gaily great—
A Shape of Ice, for the time far and dissociate.

VIII

And as the smart ship grew
In stature, grace, and hue,
In shadowy silent distance grew the Iceberg too.

IX

Alien they seemed to be:
No mortal eye could see
The intimate welding of their later history.

X

Or sign that they were bent
By paths coincident
On being anon twin halves of one august event,

XI

Till the Spinner of the Years
Said "Now!" And each one hears.
And consummation comes, and jars two hemispheres.

Thomas Hardy

A Thought

As I sit with others at a great feast, suddenly, while
   the music is playing,
To my mind, (whence it comes I know not,) spectral,
   in mist, of a wreck at sea;
Of certain ships—how they sail from port with
   flying streamers, and wafted kisses—and that is the
   last of them.

Of the solemn and murky mystery about the fate
   of the *President*;
Of the flower of the marine science of fifty generations, foundered off the Northeast course and
   going down—Of the steamship *Arctic* going down,
Of the veiled tableau—women gathered together on
deck, pale, heroic, waiting the moment that draws
   so close—O the moment!
A huge sob—a few bubbles—the white foam spirting
   up—and then the women gone,
Sinking there, while the passionless wet flows on—
   And I now pondering, Are those women indeed
   gone?
Are souls drowned and destroyed so?
Is only matter triumphant?

                                   Walt Whitman

✤ "Who's in the Next Room?"

"Who's in the next room?—who?
   I seemed to see
Somebody in the dawning passing through,
   Unknown to me."
"Nay: you saw nought. He passed invisibly."

"Who's in the next room?—who?
   I seem to hear
Somebody muttering firm in a language new
   That chills the ear."
"No: you catch not his tongue who has entered there."

"Who's in the next room?—who?
   I seem to feel
His breath like a clammy draught, as if it drew
   From the Polar Wheel."
"No, none who breathes at all does the door conceal."

"Who's in the next room?—who?
    A figure wan
With a message to one in there of something due?
    Shall I know him anon?"
"Yes he; and he brought such; and you'll know him
        anon."

Thomas Hardy

Outside and In

Suddenly I knew that you were outside the house.
The trees went silent you were prowling among,
The twigs gave warning, snapped in the evening air,
And all the birds in the garden finished singing.
What have you come for? Have you come in peace?
Or have you come to blackmail, or just to know?

And after sunset must I be made to watch
The lawn and the lane, from the bed drawn to the
        window,
The winking glass on top of the garden wall,
The shadows relaxing and stiffening under the
        moon?
I am alone, but look, I have opened the doors,
And the house is filling with cold, the winds flow in.

A house so vulnerable and divided, with
A mutiny already inside its walls,
Cannot withstand a siege. I have opened the doors
In sign of surrender. The house is filling with cold.
Why will you stay out there? I am ready to answer.
The doors are open. Why will you not come in?

Henry Reed

Ninetieth Birthday

You go up the long track
That will take a car, but is best walked
On slow feet, noting the lichen
That writes history on the page
Of the grey rock. Trees are about you
At first, but yield to the green bracken,
The nightjar's house: you can hear it spin
On warm evenings; it is still now
In the noonday heat, only the lesser
Voices sound, blue-fly and gnat
And the stream's whisper. As the road climbs,
You will pause for breath and the far sea's
Signal will flash, till you turn again
To the steep track, buttressed with cloud.

And there at the top that old woman,
Born almost a century back
In that stone farm, awaits your coming;
Waits for the news of the lost village
She thinks she knows, a place that exists
In her memory only.
                            You bring her greeting
And praise for having lasted so long
With time's knife shaving the bone.
Yet no bridge joins her own
World with yours, all you can do
Is lean kindly across the abyss
To hear words that were once wise.

R. S. Thomas

When you are Old

When you are old and grey and full of sleep,
And nodding by the fire, take down this book,
And slowly read, and dream of the soft look
Your eyes had once, and of their shadows deep;

How many loved your moments of glad grace,
And loved your beauty with love false or true,
But one man loved the pilgrim soul in you,
And loved the sorrows of your changing face;

And bending down beside the glowing bars
Murmur, a little sadly, how love fled
And paced upon the mountains overhead
And hid his face amid a crowd of stars.

William Butler Yeats

An Old Woman's Lamentations

The man I had a love for—a great rascal would kick
me in the gutter—is dead thirty years and over it, and
it is I am left behind, grey and aged. When I do be
minding the good days I had, minding what I was one
time, and what it is I'm come to, and when I do look
on my own self, poor and dry, and pinched together, it
wouldn't be much would set me raging in the streets.

John Millington Synge (from Villon)

❉ Not much Fun

"Life runs to death as to its goal, and we should go
towards that next stage of experience either carelessly
as to what must be, or with a good honest curiosity
as to what may be."

"There's not much fun in being dead, sir," said
Meehawl.

"How do you know?" said the philosopher.

James Stephens, "The Crock of Gold"

Yet we Trust

Oh yet we trust that somehow good
  Will be the final goal of ill,
  To pangs of nature, sins of will,
Defects of doubt, and taints of blood;

That nothing walks with aimless feet;
  That not one life shall be destroyed,
  Or cast as rubbish to the void,
When God hath made the pile complete;

That not a worm is cloven in vain;
  That not one moth with vain desire
  Is shrivelled in a fruitless fire,
Or but subserves another's gain.

Behold we know not anything;
  I can but trust that good shall fall
  At last—far off—at last, to all,
And every winter change to spring.

So runs my dream: but what am I?
  An infant crying in the night:
  An infant crying for the light:
And with no language but a cry.

Alfred, Lord Tennyson
(from "In Memoriam")

Crossing the Bar

Sunset and evening star,
   And one clear call for me!
And may there be no moaning of the bar,
   When I put out to sea,

But such a tide as moving seems asleep,
   Too full for sound and foam,
When that which drew from out the boundless deep
   Turns again home.

Twilight and evening bell,
   And after that the dark!
And may there be no sadness of farewell,
   When I embark;

For though from out our bourne of time and place
   The flood may bear me far,
I hope to see my pilot face to face
   When I have crost the bar.

Alfred, Lord Tennyson

He Understands the Great Cruelty of Death

My flowery and green age was passing away, and I feeling the chill in the fires had been wasting my heart, for I was drawing near the hillside that is above the grave.

The time was coming when Love and Decency can keep company, and lovers may sit together and say out all the things are in their hearts. But Death had his grudge against me, and he got in the way, like an armed robber, with a pike in his hand.

John Millington Synge (from "Petrarch")

A Form of Epitaph

Name in block letters *None that signified*
Purpose of visit *Barely ascertained*
Reasons for persevering *Hope or Pride*
Status before admission here *Regained*
Previous experience *Nil or records lost*
Requirements *Few in fact, not all unmet*
Knowledge accumulated *At a cost*
Plans *Vague* Sworn declaration *Not in debt.*

Evidence of departure *Orthodox*
Country of origin *Stateless then as now*
Securities where held *In one wood box*
Address for future reference *Below*

Is further time required? *Not the clock's*
Was permit of return petitioned? *No*
Laurence Whistler

No Coward Soul

No coward soul is mine,
No trembler in the world's storm-troubled sphere:
I see heaven's glories shine,
And faith shines equal, arming me from fear.

O God within my breast,
Almighty, ever-present Deity!
Life—that in me has rest,
As I, undying Life, have power in thee!

Vain are the thousand creeds
That move men's hearts—unutterably vain,
Worthless as withered weeds,
Or idlest froth amid the boundless main,

To waken doubt in one
Holding so fast by thy infinity;
   So surely anchored on
The steadfast rock of immortality.

   With wide-embracing love
Thy spirit animates eternal years,
   Pervades and broods above,
Changes, sustains, dissolves, creates and rears.

   Though earth and man were gone,
And suns and universes ceased to be,
   And thou were left alone,
Every existence would exist in thee.

   There is not room for death,
Nor atom that his might could render void:
   Thou—thou art Being and Breath,
And what thou art may never be destroyed.

Emily Brontë

❈ In Memory of my Mother

I do not think of you lying in the wet clay
Of a Monaghan graveyard; I see
You walking down a lane among the poplars
On your way to the station, or happily
Going to second Mass on a summer Sunday—
You meet me and you say:
"Don't forget to see about the cattle—"
Among your earthiest words the angels stray.

And I think of you walking along a headland
Of green oats in June,
So full of repose, so rich with life—

And I see us meeting at the end of a town
On a fair day by accident, after
The bargains are all made and we can walk
Together through the shops and stalls and markets
Free in the oriental streets of thought.

O you are not lying in the wet clay,
For it is a harvest evening now and we
Are piling up the ricks against the moonlight
And you smile up at us—eternally.

Patrick Kavanagh

A Point of Honour
(*In memory of Adelaide Blackburn, 1876–1962*)

You bequeathed no memorial,
But gave your body and your eyes away,
Wishing unto the last to be serviceable.
Your ashes, you said, must be scattered on Brighton
  bay
But no stone must perpetuate the trivial
Minutiae of old age that every day
Encroached on your possibilities of freedom,
Till cancer decided you could not even throw
Bread for the winter birds, or walk at random
With your companions of sunlight and casual snow.

It was snowing hard when they came to take you,
And I am told how anxious you were to dress
Neatly, yourself; it was a point of honour
To walk upright away, with your distress
Borne on your own and no one else's shoulder,
To bear with dignity your proper cross.

And then for sixteen days you were in labour,
But for yourself this time, and not for us,
Your children, who held your hand as it got darker,
As death grew large for you, but our sun less.

It is your puzzled look that I remember,
As almost gone, you caught a glimpse of me
Haunting your bedside, now a ghostly stranger
From the live world your eyes learnt not to see,
As slowly you drew from us to another
And breathless mode of being, beyond speech,
Working each night and day a little further
From sight and taste and smell and human touch,
Till you exchanged mortality, my mother,
For a new world your children could not reach.

But lying there at the end, in conversation
No longer with myself—but with the dead?—
I caught your words with interest and compassion
And when "She's wandering" the Sister said,
Thought, Yes, but with whom? for I felt on someone
Not given to my sense you attended.

And then the talking stopped. Though they continued,
Your lungs—and terribly—to labour on,
They were alone now, for the one who used them
Out of those sodden animals had gone:
So when I stood at last for the committal
Of you to death, your sediment to fire,
I did not feel the need for lamentation
Or the irrelevance of formal prayer,
Only of going on a little further
In knowledge of our dark predicament;
I think this was for you a point of honour,
And what you never said but always meant.

Thomas Blackburn

Do not go gentle into that good night

Do not go gentle into that good night,
Old age should burn and rave at close of day;
Rage, rage against the dying of the light.

Though wise men at their end know dark is right,
Because their words have forked no lightning they
Do not go gentle into that good night.

Good men, the last wave by, crying how bright
Their frail deeds might have danced in a green bay,
Rage, rage against the dying of the light.

Wild men who caught and sang the sun in flight,
And learn, too late, they grieved it on its way,
Do not go gentle into that good night.

Grave men, near death, who see with blinding sight
Blind eyes could blaze like meteors and be gay,
Rage, rage against the dying of the light.

And you, my father, there on the sad height,
Curse, bless, me now with your fierce tears, I pray.
Do not go gentle into that good night.
Rage, rage against the dying of the light.

Dylan Thomas

Portrait of a Stoic

When grief shared the front page of his life
With an emergency meeting of the Directors
And the swarming of his bees, he took the bees,
Went up for the meeting, and buried his wife.

His Directors put it down to a cold streak
In his nature, or to investments at stake,
Or an unhappy marriage. Actually, without
Intending to, he had acquired a technique.

How cool can you be? How hard can you get?
But the dust on the brim of his bowler-hat,
And a copy of *The Times*, carelessly folded,
Betrayed that in fact he was very much upset.

Not being a clubman, and having few friends,
He took the train as usual to Leatherhead,
His face a mask. Only his bees detected,
In his handling of them, that a life ends

When a wife dies. Tomorrow his bowler-hat
Will be well-brushed, his copy of *The Times*
Folded immaculately. The noble Epictetus
Would not have asked more of him than that.

F. Pratt Green

What Thomas said in a Pub

I saw God. Do you doubt it?
   Do you dare to doubt it?
I saw the Almighty Man. His hand
Was resting on a mountain. And
He looked upon the World and all about it:
I saw Him plainer that you see me now
   —You mustn't doubt it.

He was not satisfied;
   His look was all dissatisfied.

His beard swung on a wind far out of sight
Behind the world's curve. And there was light
Most fearful from His forehead. And He sighed
"That star went always wrong, and from the start
   I was dissatisfied".

He lifted up His hand—
   I say He heaved a dreadful hand
Over the spinning earth. Then I said, "Stay,
You must not strike it, God; I'm in the way;
And I will never move from where I stand".
He said, "Dear child, I feared that you were dead",
   . . . And stayed His hand.

James Stephens

God's Grandeur

The world is charged with the grandeur of God.
It will flame out, like shining from shook foil;
It gathers like a greatness, like the ooze of oil
Crushed. Why do men then now not reck his rod?
Generations have trod, have trod, have trod;
And all is seared with trade; bleared, smeared with toil;
And wears man's smudge and shares man's smell:
   the soil
Is bare now, nor can foot feel, being shod.

And for all this, nature is never spent;
There lives the dearest freshness deep down things;
And though the last lights off the black West went
Oh, morning, at the brown brink eastward, springs—
Because the Holy Ghost over the bent
World broods with warm breast and with ah!
   bright wings.

Gerard Manley Hopkins

I am the Great Sun

I am the great sun, but you do not see me,
  I am your husband, but you turn away.
I am the captive, but you do not free me,
  I am the captain you will not obey.

I am the truth, but you will not believe me,
  I am the city where you will not stay,
I am your wife, your child, but you will leave me,
  I am that God to whom you will not pray.

I am your counsel, but you do not hear me,
  I am the lover whom you will betray,
I am the victor, but you do not cheer me,
  I am the holy dove whom you will slay.

I am your life, but if you will not name me,
Seal up your soul with tears, and never blame me.
Charles Causley

The Kingdom of God

O world invisible, we view thee,
O world intangible, we touch thee,
O world unknowable, we know thee,
Inapprehensible, we clutch thee!

Does the fish soar to find the ocean,
The eagle plunge to find the air—
That we ask of the stars in motion
If they have rumour of thee there?

Not where the wheeling systems darken,
And our benumbed conceiving soars!—
The drift of pinions, would we hearken,
Beats at our own clay-shuttered doors.

The angels keep their ancient places;—
Turn but a stone, and start a wing!
'Tis ye, 'tis your estrangèd faces,
That miss the many-splendoured thing.

But (when so sad thou canst not sadder)
Cry—and upon thy so sore loss
Shall shine the traffic of Jacob's ladder
Pitched betwixt Heaven and Charing Cross.

Yea, in the night, my Soul, my daughter,
Cry—clinging Heaven by the hems;
And lo, Christ walking on the water
Not of Gennesareth, but Thames!

Francis Thompson

Who is at my Window?

Who is at my window? Who? Who?
Go from my window! Go! Go!
Who calls there, like a stranger,
Go from my window! Go!

—Lord, I am here, a wretched mortal,
That for thy mercy doth cry and call
Unto thee, my lord celestial,
See who is at thy window, who?—

Remember thy sin, remember thy smart,
And also for thee what was my part,
Remember the spear that pierced my heart,
And in at my door thou shalt go.

I ask no thing of thee therefore,
But love for love, to lay in store.
Give me thy heart; I ask no more,
And in at my door thou shalt go.

Who is at my window? Who?
Go from my window! Go!
Cry no more there, like a stranger,
But in at my door thou go!

Anonymous (c. 1500)

From the Ballad of Reading Gaol

I never saw a man who looked
　　With such a wistful eye
Upon that little tent of blue
We prisoners call the sky,
　　And at every careless cloud that passed
　　　In happy freedom by.

The Warders strutted up and down
　　And kept their herd of brutes,
Their uniforms were spick and span,
　　And they wore their Sunday suits,
But we knew the work that they'd been at,
　　By the quicklime on their boots.

For where a grave had opened wide,
   There was no grave at all:
Only a stretch of mud and sand
   By the hideous prison-wall,
And a little heap of burning lime
     That the man should have his pall.

For he has a pall, this wretched man,
   Such as few men can claim:
Deep down below a prison-yard,
   Naked for greater shame,
He lies with fetters on each foot
     Wrapt in a sheet of flame!

And all the while the burning lime
   Eats flesh and bone away,
It eats the brittle bone by night,
   And the soft flesh day by day,
It eats the flesh and bone by turns,
     And it eats the heart away.

For three long years they will not sow
   Or root or seedling there:
For three long years the unblessed spot
   Will sterile be and bare,
And look upon the wondering sky
     With unreproachful stare.

They think a murderer's heart would taint
   Each simple seed they sow.
It is not true! God's kindly earth
   Is kindlier than men know,
And the red rose would but blow more red,
     The white rose whiter blow.

Oscar Wilde

The Day Larry was Stretched

The dawn they did Larry the speckled dust
lifted a twisted curtain round
the whistler corner and creased papers
danced to the chill of a street wind.

Over the gutters the leching sparrows
pick-axed an hour grey as a hat
with early caring, and blue pigeons
clattered soft drums on the monument.

A yellow of lemons and child's ribbons
stroked a slate skyline; upon its wall
willow herb whipped a flicker of stem
to a storm of seed through a blitzed school.

A door slammed hollow, the glass clangours
of blue steel crates down the mild-washed street
turned over the sleepers. A mild policeman
flicked at the dust on his mirror boots.

At the island of farm in a sea of suburb
the cock stretched its neck in a raw scream
friendly as traffic. The empty station
blew papers after the first train.

The dawn they did Larry the rain scattered
pocks on the river, specks of lead
stinging the smooth, and an old jacket
drifted downtide like a drowned god.

Robin Skelton

❧ Day of these Days

Such a morning it is when love
leans through geranium windows
and calls with a cockerel's tongue.

When red-haired girls scamper like roses
over the rain-green grass,
and the sun drips honey.

When hedgerows grow venerable,
berries dry black as blood,
and holes suck in their bees.

Such a morning it is when mice
run whispering from the church,
dragging dropped ears of harvest.

When the partridge draws back his spring
and shoots like a buzzing arrow
over grained and mahogany fields.

When no table is bare
and no bread dry
and the tramp feeds off ribs of rabbit.

Such a day it is when time
piles up the hills like pumpkins
and the streams run golden.

When all men smell good,
and the cheeks of girls
are as baked bread to the mouth.

As bread and bean flowers
the touch of their lips,
and their white teeth sweeter than cucumbers.

Laurie Lee

Everyone Sang

Everyone suddenly burst out singing;
And I was filled with such delight
As prisoned birds must find in freedom
Winging wildly across the white
Orchards and dark green fields; on; on; and out of
    sight.

Everyone's voice was suddenly lifted,
And beauty came like the setting sun.
My heart was shaken with tears and horror
Drifted away. . . . O but every one
Was a bird; and the song was wordless; the singing
    will never be done.

Siegfried Sassoon

Snatch of Sliphorn Jazz

Are you happy? It's the only way to be, kid.
Yes, be happy, it's a good nice way to be.
But not happy-happy, kid, don't
be too doubled-up doggone happy.
It's the doubled-up doggone happy-
happy people . . . bust hard . . . they
do bust hard . . . when they bust.
Be happy, kid, go to it, but not too
doggone happy.

Carl Sandburg

❊ Holiday Memory

August Bank Holiday. A tune on an ice-cream cornet. A slap of sea and a tickle of sand. A fanfare of sunshades opening. A wince and whinny of bathers dancing into deceptive water. A tuck of dresses. A rolling of trousers. A compromise of paddlers. A sunburn of girls and a lark of boys. A silent hullabaloo of balloons.

I remember the sea telling lies in a shell held to my ear for a whole harmonious, hollow minute by a small, wet girl in an enormous bathing-suit marked 'Corporation property'.

I remember sharing the last of my moist buns with a boy and a lion. Tawny and savage, with cruel nails and capacious mouth, the little boy tore and devoured. Wild as seed-cake, ferocious as a hearth-rug, the depressed and verminous lion nibbled like a mouse at his half a bun, and hiccupped in the sad dusk of his cage.

I remember a man like an alderman or a bailiff, bowlered and collarless, with a bag of monkey-nuts in his hand, crying "Ride 'em, cowboy!" time and again as he whirled in his chairoplane giddily above the upturned laughing faces of the town girls bold as brass and the boys with padded shoulders and shoes as sharp as knives; and the monkey-nuts flew through the air like salty hail.

Children all day capered or squealed by the glazed or bashing sea, and the steam-organ wheezed its waltzes in the threadbare playground and the waste lot, where the dodgems dodged, behind the pickle factory.

And mothers loudly warned their proud pink
daughters or sons to put that jellyfish down; and
fathers spread newspapers over their faces; and sand-
fleas hopped on the picnic lettuce; and someone had
forgotten the salt.

In those always radiant, rainless, lazily rowdy and
sky-blue summers departed, I remember August
Monday from the rising of the sun over the stained
and royal town to the husky hushing of the round-
about music and the dowsing of the naphtha jets in
the seaside fair: from bubble-and-squeak to the last
of the sandy sandwiches.

Dylan Thomas

Trebetherick

We used to picnic where the thrift
Grew deep and tufted to the edge;
We saw the yellow foam-flakes drift
In trembling sponges on the ledge
Below us, till the wind would lift
Them up the cliff and o'er the hedge.
Sand in the sandwiches, wasps in the tea,
Sun on our bathing-dresses heavy with wet,
Squelch of the bladder-wrack waiting for sea,
Fleas round the tamarisk, an early cigarette.

From where the coastguard houses stood
One used to see, below the hill,
The lichened branches of a wood
In summer silver-cool and still;
And there the Shade of Evil could
Stretch out at us from Shilla Mill.

Thick with sloe and blackberry, uneven in the light,
Lonely ran the hedge, the heavy meadow was
    remote,
The oldest part of Cornwall was the wood as black
    as night,
And the pheasant and the rabbit lay torn open at
    the throat.

But when a storm was at its height,
And feathery slate was black in rain,
And tamarisks were hung with light
And golden sand was brown again,
Spring tide and blizzard would unite
And sea come flooding up the lane.
Waves full of treasure then were roaring up the
    beach,
Ropes round our mackintoshes, waders warm and
    dry,
We waited for the wreckage to come swirling into
    reach,
Ralph, Vasey, Alastair, Biddy, John and I.

Then roller into roller curled
And thundered down the rocky bay,
And we were in a water-world
Of rain and blizzard, sea and spray,
And one against the other hurled
We struggled round to Greenaway.
Blesséd be St. Enodoc, blesséd be the wave,
Blesséd be the springy turf, we pray, pray to thee,
Ask for our children all the happy days you gave
To Ralph, Vasey, Alastair, Biddy, John and me.

John Betjeman

After Apple-picking

My long two-pointed ladder's sticking through a tree
Toward heaven still,
And there's a barrel that I didn't fill
Beside it, and there may be two or three
Apples I didn't pick upon some bough.
But I am done with apple-picking now,
Essence of winter sleep is on the night,
The scent of apples: I am drowsing off.
I cannot rub the strangeness from my sight
I got from looking through a pane of glass
I skimmed this morning from the drinking trough
And held against the world of hoary grass.
It melted, and I let it fall and break.
But I was well
Upon my way to sleep before it fell,
And I could tell
What form my dreaming was about to take.
Magnified apples appear and disappear,
Stem end and blossom end,
And every fleck of russet showing clear.
My instep arch not only keeps the ache,
It keeps the pressure of a ladder-round.
I feel the ladder sway as the boughs bend.
And I keep hearing from the cellar bin
The rumbling sound
Of load on load of apples coming in.
For I have had too much
Of apple-picking: I am overtired
Of the great harvest I myself desired.
There were ten thousand fruit to touch,
Cherish in hand, lift down, and not let fall.
For all
That struck the earth,
No matter if not bruised or spiked with stubble,

Went surely to the cider-apple heap
As of no worth.
One can see what will trouble
This sleep of mine, whatever sleep it is.
Were he not gone,
The woodchuck could say whether it's like his
Long sleep, as I describe its coming on,
Or just some human sleep.

Robert Frost

Weary with Toil

Weary with toil, I haste me to my bed,
The dear repose for limbs with travel tired,
But then begins a journey in my head
To work my mind, when body's work's expired.
For then my thoughts (from far where I abide)
Intend a zealous pilgrimage to thee,
And keep my drooping eyelids open wide,
Looking on darkness which the blind do see.
Save that my soul's imaginary sight
Presents thy shadow to my sightless view,
Which like a jewel (hung in ghastly night)
Makes black night beauteous, and her old face new.
Lo thus by day my limbs, by night my mind,
For thee, and for myself, no quiet find.

William Shakespeare

To Dream Again

Be not afeard, the isle is full of noises,
Sounds, and sweet airs, that give delight and hurt
   not;
Sometimes a thousand twangling instruments
Will hum about mine ears; and sometimes voices,
That, if I then had waked after long sleep,
Will make me sleep again: and then, in dreaming,
The clouds methought would open, and show riches
Ready to drop upon me, that when I waked
I cried to dream again.

William Shakespeare
(The Tempest)

For a Sleeper

Minute-hand and moon and mind,
Turning in a windless night,
Gather moment as the light
Halts before your window-blind.

Over clockface, field and farm,
Narrows the sector of the dark
Till springing into light, a lark
Touches-off the day's alarm.

Paul Dehn

❈ The Starlight Night

Look at the stars! look, look up at the skies!
  O look at all the fire-folk sitting in the air!
  The bright boroughs, the circle-citadels there!
Down in dim woods the diamond delves! the elves'-
    eyes!

The grey lawns cold where gold, where quickgold
    lies!
  Wind-beat whitebeam! airy abeles set on a flare!
  Flake-doves sent floating forth at a farmyard
    scare!—
Ah well! it is all a purchase, all is a prize.

Buy then! bid then!—What?—Prayer, patience,
    alms, vows.
Look, look: a May-mess, like on orchard boughs!
  Look! March-blown, like on mealed-with-yellow
    sallows!
These are indeed the barn; withindoors house
The shocks. This piece-bright paling shuts the
    spouse
  Christ home, Christ and His mother and all His
    hallows.

Gerard Manley Hopkins

The Sunlight on the Garden

The sunlight on the garden
Hardens and grows cold,
We cannot cage the minute
Within its nets of gold,
When all is told
We cannot beg for pardon.

Our freedom as free lances
Advances towards its end;
The earth compels, upon it
Sonnets and birds descend;
And soon, my friend,
We shall have no time for dances.

The sky was good for flying
Defying the church bells
And every evil iron
Siren and what it tells:
The earth compels,
*We are dying, Egypt, dying

And not expecting pardon,
Hardened in heart anew,
But glad to have sat under
Thunder and rain with you,
And grateful too
For sunlight on the garden.

Louis MacNeice

Shancoduff

My black hills have never seen the sun rising,
Eternally they look north towards Armagh.
Lot's wife would not be salt if she had been
Incurious as my black hills that are happy
When dawn whitens Glassdrummond chapel.

My hills hoard the bright shillings of March
While the sun searches in every pocket.
They are my Alps and I have climbed the
        Matterhorn
With a sheaf of hay for three perishing calves
In the field under the big Forth of Rocksavage.

* The last words spoken by Antony in Shakespeare's *Antony and Cleopatra.*

The sleety winds fondle the rushy beards of
    Shancoduff
While the cattle-drovers sheltering in the Featherna
    Bush
Look up and say: "Who owns them hungry hills
That the water-hen and snipe must have forsaken?
A poet? Then by heavens he must be poor"
I hear and is my heart not bitterly shaken?

Patrick Kavanagh

Part 2

❖ Lord Randal

"O where ha you been, Lord Randal, my son?
And where ha you been, my handsome young
   man?"
"I ha been at the greenwood; mother, mak my bed
   soon,
For I'm wearied wi huntin, and fain wad lie down."

"An wha met ye there, Lord Randal, my son?
An wha met you there, my handsome young man?"
"O I met wi my true-love; mother, mak my bed
   soon,
For I'm wearied wi huntin, and fain wad lie down."

"And what did she give you, Lord Randal, my
   son?
And what did she give you, my handsome young
   man?"
"Eels fried in a pan; mother, mak my bed soon,
For I'm wearied wi huntin, and fain wad lie down."

"And wha gat your leavins, Lord Randal, my son?
And wha gat your leavins, my handsome young
   man?"
"My hawks and my hounds; mother, mak my bed
   soon,
For I'm wearied wi huntin, and fain wad lie down."

"And what becam of them, Lord Randal, my son?
And what becam of them, my handsome young
    man?"
"They stretched their legs out and died; mother,
    mak my bed soon,
For I'm wearied wi huntin, and fain wad lie down."

"O I fear you are poisoned, Lord Randal, my son!
I fear you are poisoned, my handsome young
    man!"
"O yes, I am poisoned; mother, mak my bed soon,
For I'm sick at the heart, and I fain wad lie down."

"What d' ye leave to your mother, Lord Randal,
    my son?
What d' ye leave to your mother, my handsome
    young man?"
"Four and twenty milk kye; mother, mak my bed
    soon.
For I'm sick at the heart, and I fain wad lie down."

'What d' ye leave to your sister, Lord Randal, my
    son?
What d' ye leave to your sister, my handsome
    young man?"
"My gold and my silver; mother, mak my bed soon,
For I'm sick at the heart, and I fain wad lie down."

"What d' ye leave to your brother, Lord Randal, my
    son?
What d' ye leave to your brother, my handsome
    young man?"
"My houses and my lands; mother, mak my bed
    soon,
For I'm sick at the heart, and I fain wad lie down."

Danny

One night a score of Errismen,
A score I'm told and nine,
Said, "We'll get shut of Danny's noise
Of girls and widows dyin'.

"There's not his like from Binghamstown
To Boyle and Ballycroy,
At playing hell on decent girls,
At beating man and boy.

"He's left two pairs of female twins
Beyond in Killacreest,
And twice in Crossmolina fair
He's struck the parish priest.

"But we'll come round him in the night
A mite beyond the Mullet;
Ten will quench his bloody eyes
And ten will choke his gullet."

It wasn't long till Danny came,
From Bangor making way,
And he was damning moon and stars
And whistling grand and gay.

Till in a gap of hazel glen—
And not a hare in sight—
Out legged the nine-and-twenty lads
Along his left and right.

Then Danny smashed the nose on Byrne,
He split the lips on three,
And bit across the right-hand thumb
Of one Red Shawn Magee.

But seven tripped him up behind,
And seven kicked before,
And seven squeezed around his throat
Till Danny kicked no more.

Then some destroyed him with their heels,
Some tramped him in the mud,
Some stole his purse and timber pipe,
And some washed off his blood.

And when you're walking out the way
From Bangor to Balmullet,
You'll see a flat cross on a stone
Where men choked Danny's gullet.

J. M. Synge

❖ Farewell to Old England

Farewell to old England for ever,
Farewell to our rum-culls* as well;
Farewell to the well-loved Old Bailey
Where I used for to cut such a swell.

Singing too-ra-lie, too-ra-lie, addity,
Singing too-ra-lie, too-ra-lie, aye,
Singing too-ra-lie, too-ra-lie, addity,
We're sailing for Botany Bay.

'Taint leaving Old England we cares about,
'Taint 'cause we mis-spells what we knows;
But because we light-fingered gentry
Hops around with a log on our toes.

* pals

There's the captain as is our commandier,
There's the bosun and all the ship's crew,
There's the first and the second class passengers
Knows what we poor convicts goes through.

For fourteen long years I'm transported,
For fourteen long years and a day,
Just for meeting a cove in the alley,
And stealing his ticker away.

Oh, had I the wings of a turtle-dove!
I'd soar on my pinions so high;
Slap bang to the arms of my Polly-love,
And in her sweet bosom I'd die.

Now, all you young dukies and duchesses,
Take warning from what I do say,
Mind, all is your own as you touchesses,
Or you'll meet us in Botany Bay.

Anonymous

The Greenwich Prisoner

'Twas in the good ship *Rover*,
I sailed the world all round,
And for three years and over
I ne'er touched British ground,
At length in England landed
I left the roaring main,
Found all relations stranded,
And went to see again,
And went to sea again.

That time bound straight for Portugal,
Right fore and aft we bore,
But when we made Cape Ortegal,
A gale blew off the shore;

She lay, so did it shock her,
A log upon the main,
Till, saved from Davey's locker,
We put to sea again,
We put to sea again.

Next sailing in a frigate
I got my timber toe.
I never more shall jig it
As once I used to do;
My leg was shot off fairly,
All by a ship of Spain;
But I could swab a galley,
I went to sea again,
I went to sea again.

And still I am enabled
To bring up in the rear,
Although I'm quite disabled
And lie in Greenwich tier.
There's schooners in the river
A-riding to the chain,
But I shall never, ever
Put out to sea again,
Put out to sea again.

Anonymous

❋ The Castle

All through that summer at ease we lay,
And daily from the turret wall
We watched the mowers in the hay
And the enemy half a mile away.
They seemed no threat to us at all.

For what, we thought, had we to fear
With our arms and provender, load on load,
Our towering battlements, tier on tier,
And friendly allies drawing near
On every leafy summer road.

Our gates were strong, our walls were thick,
So smooth and high, no man could win
A foothold there, no clever trick
Could take us, have us dead or quick.
Only a bird could have got in.

What could they offer us for a bait?
Our captain was brave, and we were true. . . .
There was a little private gate,
A little wicked wicket gate.
The wizened warder let them through.

Oh then the maze of tunnelled stone
Grew thin and treacherous as air.
The cause was lost without a groan,
The famous citadel overthrown,
And all its secret galleries bare.

How can this shameful tale be told?
I will maintain until my death
We could do nothing, being sold;
Our only enemy was gold,
And we had no arms to fight it with.

Edwin Muir

Two Wise Generals

"Not as Black Douglas, bannered, trumpeted,
Who hacked for the casked heart flung to the enemy,
Letting the whole air flow breakneck with blood
Till he fell astride that handful, you and I

Come, two timid and ageing generals
To parley, and to divide the territory
Upon a map, and get honour, and by
This satisfaction part with regiments whole."

They entered the lit tent, in no hurry to grab.
Apart in darkness twinkled their armies
Like two safe towns. Thus they drank, joked, waxed
    wise—
So heavily medalled never need fear stab.

The treaty sealed, lands allotted (and a good third
Stuffed down their tunic fronts' private estate)
They left the empty bottle. The tent-lamp out,
They lurched away in the knee-high mist, hearing
    the first bird,

Towards separate camps. Now, one a late dew-moth
Eyes, as he sways, among the still tents. The other
    roars "Guard!"
As a fox ducks from the silent parapet. Both
Have found their sleeping armies massacred.

Ted Hughes

The High Tide on the Coast of Lincolnshire, 1571

The old mayor climbed the belfry tower,
  The ringers ran by two, by three;
"Pull, if ye never pulled before;
  Good ringers, pull your best," quoth he.
"Play up, play up, O Boston bells!
Play all your changes, all your swells,
Play up 'The Brides of Enderby'!"

Men say it was a stolen tide—
  The Lord that sent it, He knows all;
But in mine ears doth still abide
  The message that the bells let fall:
And there was naught of strange, beside
The flights of mews* and peewits pied,
  By millions crouched on the old sea-wall.

I sat and spun within the door,
  My thread brake off, I raised mine eyes;
The level sun, like ruddy ore,
  Lay sinking in the barren skies;
And dark against day's golden death
She moved where Lindis wandereth,
  My son's fair wife, Elizabeth.

"Cusha! Cusha! Cusha!" calling,
Ere the early dews were falling,
  Far away I heard her song,
  "Cusha! Cusha!" all along,
Where the reedy Lindis floweth,
    Floweth, floweth,
From the meads where melick groweth,
  Faintly came her milking-song.

* gulls

"Cusha! Cusha! Cusha!" calling,
"For the dews will soon be falling;
　　Leave your meadow grasses mellow,
　　　　Mellow, mellow;
　　Quit your cowslips, cowslips yellow;
Come up, Whitefoot; come up, Lightfoot;
　　Quit the stalks of parsley hollow,
　　　　Hollow, hollow;
Come up, Jetty, rise and follow,
　　From the clovers lift your head;
Come up, Whitefoot; come up, Lightfoot;
Come up, Jetty, rise and follow,
　　Jetty, to the milking-shed."

If it be long, aye, long ago,
　　When I begin to think how long,
Again I hear the Lindis flow,
　　Swift as an arrow, sharp and strong;
And all the air, it seemeth me,
Bin full of floating bells (saith she)
That ring the tune of Enderby.

All fresh the level pasture lay,
　　And not a shadow might be seen,
Save where full five good miles away
　　The steeple towered from out the green;
And lo! the great bell far and wide
Was heard in all the countryside
That Saturday at eventide.

The swanherds where their sedges* are
　　Moved on in sunset's golden breath,
The shepherd lads I heard afar,
　　And my son's wife, Elizabeth;

* reeds

94

Till floating o'er the grassy sea
Came down that kindly message free,
"The Brides of Mavis Enderby."

Then some looked up into the sky,
   And all along where Lindis flows
To where the goodly vessels lie,
   And where the lordly steeple shows.
They said, "And why should this thing be?
What danger lowers by land or sea?
They ring the tune of Enderby!

"For evil news from Mablethorpe,
   Of pirate galleys warping down;
For ships ashore beyond the scorpe,*
   They have not spared to wake the town;
But while the west bin red to see,
And storms be none, and pirates flee,
Why ring 'The Brides of Enderby'?"

I looked without, and lo! my son
   Came riding down with might and main:
He raised a shout as he drew on,
   Till all the welkin† rang again,
"Elizabeth! Elizabeth!"
(A sweeter woman ne'er drew breath
Than my son's wife, Elizabeth.)

"The old sea-wall" (he cried) "is down,
   The rising tide comes on apace,
And boats adrift in yonder town
   Go sailing up the market-place."
He shook as one that looks on death:
"God save you, mother!" straight he saith;
"Where is my wife, Elizabeth?"

* cliff   † sky

"Good son, where Lindis winds away,
    With her two bairns I marked her long;
And ere yon bells began to play,
    Afar I heard her milking-song."
He looked across the grassy sea,
To right, to left, "Ho, Enderby!"
They rang "The Brides of Enderby!"

With that he cried and beat his breast;
    For lo! along the river's bed
A mighty eygre* reared his crest,
    And up the Lindis raging sped.
It swept with thunderous noises loud;
Shaped like a curling, snow-white cloud,
Or like a demon in a shroud.

And rearing Lindis backward pressed,
    Shook all her trembling banks amain;
Then madly at the eygre's breast
    Flung up her weltering walls again.
Then banks came down with ruin and rout—
Then beaten foam flew round about—
Then all the mighty floods were out.

So far, so fast the eygre drave,
    The heart had hardly time to beat
Before a shallow, seething wave
    Sobbed in the grasses at our feet;
The feet had hardly time to flee
Before it brake against the knee,
And all the world was in the sea.

Upon the roof we sat that night,
    The noise of bells went sweeping by;
I marked the lofty beacon light
    Stream from the church-tower, red and high—

* flood wave

A lurid mark and dread to see;
And awesome bells they were to me,
 That in the dark rang "Enderby".

They rang the sailor lads to guide
  From roof to roof who fearless rowed;
And I—my son was at my side,
  And yet the ruddy beacon glowed:
And yet he moaned beneath his breath,
"O come in life, or come in death!
O lost! my love, Elizabeth."

And didst thou visit him no more?
  Thou didst, thou didst, my daughter dear!
The waters laid thee at his door,
  Ere yet the early dawn was clear.
Thy pretty bairns in fast embrace,
The lifted sun shone on thy face,
Down drifted to thy dwelling-place.

That flow strewed wrecks about the grass;
  That ebb swept out the flocks to sea;
A fatal ebb and flow, alas!
  To many more than mine and me:
But each will mourn his own (she saith),
And sweeter woman ne'er drew breath
Than my son's wife, Elizabeth.

  I shall never hear her more
   By the reedy Lindis shore,
"Cusha! Cusha! Cusha!" calling,
Ere the early dews be falling;
I shall never hear her song,
"Cusha! Cusha!" all along,
Where the reedy Lindis floweth,
    Goeth, floweth;

From the meads where melick groweth,
When the water, winding down,
Onward floweth to the town.

I shall never see her more
Where the reeds and rushes quiver,
    Shiver, quiver;
Stand beside the sobbing river,
Sobbing, throbbing, in its falling
To the sandy, lonesome shore;
I shall never hear her calling,
"Leave your meadow grasses mellow,
    Mellow, mellow;
Quit your cowslips, cowslips yellow;
Come up, Whitefoot; come up, Lightfoot;
Quit your pipes of parsley hollow,
    Hollow, hollow;
Come up, Lightfoot, rise and follow:
    Lightfoot, Whitefoot,
  From your clovers lift the head;
Come up, Jetty, follow, follow,
  Jetty, to the milking-shed."

Jean Ingelow

The Death of Samson

Occasions drew me early to this city,
And as the gates I entered with sunrise,
The morning trumpets festival proclaimed
Through each high street. Little I had dispatched,
When all abroad was rumoured, that this day
Samson should be brought forth to show the people,
Proof of his mighty strength in feats and games;
I sorrowed at his captive state, but minded
Not to be absent at that spectacle.

The building was a spacious theatre,
Half-round, on two main pillars vaulted high,
With seats, where all the lords and each degree
Of sort might sit in order to behold;
The other side was open, where the throng
On banks and scaffolds under sky might stand;
I among these aloof obscurely stood.
The feast and noon grew high, and sacrifice
Had filled their hearts with mirth, high cheer, and
    wine,
When to their sports they turned. Immediately
Was Samson as a public servant brought,
In their state livery clad; before him pipes
And timbrels, on each side went armed guards,
Both horse and foot, before him and behind
Archers, and slingers, cataphracts,* and spears.
At sight of him the people with a shout
Rifted the air, clamouring their god with praise,
Who had made their dreadful enemy their thrall.
He patient, but undaunted, where they led him,
Came to the place, and what was set before him,
Which without help of eye might be assayed,
To heave, pull, draw, or break, he still performed,
All with incredible stupendous force,
None daring to appear antagonist.
At length, for intermission sake, they led him
Between the pillars; he his guide requested,
For so from such as nearer stood we heard,
As over-tired, to let him lean awhile
With both his arms on those two massy pillars,
That to the arched roof gave main support.
He, unsuspicious, led him; which when Samson
Felt in his arms, with head awhile inclined,
And eyes fast fixed he stood, as one who prayed,

* soldiers in armour

Or some great matter in his mind revolved:
At last, with head erect, thus cried aloud:
"Hitherto, lords, what your commands imposed
I have performed, as reason was, obeying,
Not without wonder or delight beheld:
Now of my own accord, such other trial
I mean to show you of my strength, yet greater;
As with amaze shall strike all who behold".
This uttered, straining all his nerves, he bowed.
As with the force of winds and waters pent,
When mountains tremble, those two massy pillars
With horrible convulsion to and fro
He tugged, he shook, till down they came, and drew
The whole roof after them, with burst of thunder,
Upon the heads of all who sat beneath,
Lords, ladies, captains, counsellors, or priests
Their choice nobility and flower, not only
Of this, but each Philistian city round,
Met from all parts to solemnize this feast.
Samson, with these inmixed, inevitably
Pulled down the same destruction on himself.

John Milton
from "Samson Agonistes"

❊ The Orphan's Song

I had a little bird,
I took it from the nest;
I prest it, and blest it,
And nurst it in my breast.

I set it on the ground,
I danced round and round,
And sang about it so cheerly,
With "Hey my little bird, and ho my little bird,
And ho but I love thee dearly!"

I make a little feast
Of food soft and sweet,
I hold it in my breast,
And coax it to eat;

I pit, and I pat,
I call it this and that,
And sing about it so cheerly,
With "Hey my little bird, and ho my little bird,
And ho but I love thee dearly!"

I may kiss, I may sing,
But I can't make it feed,
It taketh no heed
Of any pleasant thing.

I scolded and I socked,
But it minded not a whit,
Its little mouth was locked,
And I could not open it.

Tho' with pit, and with pat,
And with this, and with that,
I sang about it so cheerly,
With "Hey my little bird, and ho my little bird,
And ho but I love thee dearly!"

But when the day was done,
And the room was at rest,
And I sat all alone
With my birdie in my breast,

And the light had fled,
And not a sound was heard,
Then my little bird
Lifted up its head,

And the little mouth
Loosed its sullen pride,
And it opened, it opened,
With a yearning strong and wide.

Swifter than I speak
I brought it food once more,
But the poor little beak
Was locked as before.

I sat down again,
And not a creature stirred;
I laid the little bird
Again where it had laid;

And again when nothing stirred,
And not a word I said,
Then my little bird
Lifted up its head,

And the little beak
Loosed its stubborn pride,
And it opened, it opened,
With a yearning strong and wide.

It lay in my breast,
It uttered no cry,
'Twas famished, 'twas famished,
And I couldn't tell why.

I couldn't tell why,
But I saw that it would die,
For all that I kept dancing round and round,
And singing about it so cheerly,
With "Hey my little bird, and ho my little bird,
And ho but I love thee dearly!"

I never look sad,
I hear what people say,
I laugh when they are gay
And they think I am glad.

My tears never start,
I never say a word,
But I think that my heart
Is like that little bird.

Every day I read,
And I sing, and I play,
But thro' the long day
It taketh no heed.

It taketh no heed
Of any pleasant thing,
I know it doth not read,
I know it doth not sing.

With my mouth I read,
With my hands I play,
My shut heart is shut,
Coax it how you may.

You may coax it how you may
While the day is broad and bright,
But in the dead night
When the guests are gone away,

And no more the music sweet
Up the house doth pass,
Nor the dancing feet
Shake the nursery glass;

And I've heard my aunt
Along the corridor,
And my uncle gaunt
Lock his chamber door;

And upon the stair
All is hushed and still,
And the last wheel
Is silent in the square;

And the nurses snore,
And the dim sheets rise and fall,
And the lamplight's on the wall,
And the mouse is on the floor;

And the curtains of my bed
Are like a heavy cloud,
And the clock ticks loud,
And the sounds are in my head;

And little Lizzie sleeps
Softly at my side,
And it opens, it opens,
With a yearning strong and wide.

It yearns in my breast,
It utters no cry,
'Tis famished, 'tis famished,
And I feel that I shall die,
I feel that I shall die,
And none will know why.

Tho' the pleasant life is dancing round and round,
And singing about me so cheerly,
With "Hey my little bird, and ho my little bird,
And ho but I love thee dearly!"

Sydney Dobell

Death of a Bird

After those first days
When we had placed him in his iron cage
  And made a space for him
    From such

  Outrageous cage of wire,
Long and shallow, where the sunlight fell
  Through the air, onto him;
    After

  He had been fed for three days
Suddenly, in that sunlight before noon,
  He was dead with no
    Pretence.

  He did not say goodbye,
He did not say thankyou, but he died then
  Lying flat on the rigid
    Wires

  Of his cage, his gold
Beak shut tight, which once in hunger had
  Opened as a trap
    And then

  Swiftly closed again,
Swallowing quickly what I had given him;
  How can I say I am sorry
    He died.

  Seeing him lie there dead,
Death's friend with death, I was angry he
  Had gone without pretext or warning,
    With no

Suggestion first he should go,
Since I had fed him, then put wires round him,
    Bade him hop across
        The bars of my hands.

    I asked him only that
He should desire his life. He had become
    Of us a black friend with
        A gold mouth

    Shrilly singing through
The heat. The labour of the black bird! I
    Cannot understand why
        He is dead.

I bury him familiarly.
His heritage is a small brown garden.
Something is added to the everlasting earth;
From my mind a space is taken away.

John Silkin

✳ The Burial of Sir John Moore

Not a drum was heard, not a funeral note,
    As his corse* to the rampart we hurried;
Not a soldier discharged his farewell shot
    O'er the grave where our hero we buried.

We buried him darkly at dead of night,
    The sods with our bayonets turning,
By the struggling moonbeam's misty light,
    And the lantern dimly burning.

* corpse

No useless coffin enclosed his breast,
    Not in sheet nor in shroud we wound him;
But he lay like a warrior taking his rest
    With his martial cloak around him.

Few and short were the prayers we said,
    And we spoke not a word of sorrow:
But we steadfastly gazed on the face that was dead,
    And we bitterly thought of the morrow.

We thought, as we hollowed his narrow bed,
    And smoothed down his lonely pillow,
That the foe and the stranger would tread o'er his
        head,
    And we far away on the billow!

Lightly they'll talk of the spirit that's gone,
And o'er his cold ashes upbraid him;
But little he'll reck,* if they let him sleep on,
    In the grave where a Briton has laid him.

But half of our heavy task was done,
    When the clock struck the hour for retiring;
And we heard the distant and random gun
    That the foe was sullenly firing.

Slowly and sadly we laid him down
    From the field of his fame fresh and gory;
We carved not a line, and we raised not a stone—
    But we left him alone with his glory.
                                    Charles Wolfe

* heed

Elegy for a Lost Submarine
H.M.S. Affray: Lost 16th April, 1951

The Prologue

Would you talk to Davy Jones in his locker?
Put your earphones on and talk to Davy Jones!
Would you talk to Davy Jones,
With his sea-chest full of bones—
    We are bound to mention bones
    When we think of Davy Jones—
With your asdic sets, your radar and your deepsea
  telephones,
Would you talk to Davy Jones in his locker?

TAP TAP TAP TAP
TAP TAP TAP TAP

    For K 5. Off the Scillies, 57 dead.
    For H 24. Near Gibraltar, 43 dead.
    For L 24. Off Portland, 43 dead.
    For M 1. Off Start Point, 68 dead.
    For H 29. In Devonport Dock, 6 dead.
    For H 7. Off the Pembroke coast, 24 dead.
    For Poseidon. In the China Seas, 20 dead.
    For M 2. Off Portland, 60 dead.
    For Thetis. In Liverpool Bay, 99 dead.
    For Truculent. In the Thames Estuary, 64 dead.
    For Affray. Off Alderney, 75 dead.

For these, lost in peace-time, on manoeuvres, on
    their trials, on training cruises, lost, rammed,
    sunk in dock, disappeared.

For all these, drumtaps and the slow drumbeat:
    Drumtaps and the piping whistles shrill and
        shrilling,

At the service never-ending, at the burial of
   the dead;

TAP TAP TAP TAP
TAP TAP TAP TAP

And in war? How many?
What chorus of silent ships, all told,
And past, present, and to come?

TAP TAP TAP TAP
TAP TAP TAP TAP

The Elegy

Red sails in the sunset, white plume of a smokestack,
Ironclad or clipper, submarine or barge,
Whatever her name and rig the ship is always SHE;
At times, the best of women,
Then again, uncertain, coy and hard to please;
Ocean Queen to the Ocean's King,
His decoy, or his cockle plaything;
So somewhere between the Needles and Portland
   Bill,
She dived; there was a strong tide and the wind
   was gunning,
In April, with the snow still on the Northumbrian
   fells,
She dived; and it was night and it was morning.

Night of black depthless depths, long, long night,
Your waters will not divide again,
Nor her keen bisecting sides play dolphin, surfacing!
How shall we filter and find, grey shadowy morning,
Lift and count these bodies, close these eyes?

Here, as a sun we do not feel breaks through your
   mists,
The face on the sea's cold mirror is our own.
Sending out the supersonic signals,
Searching the wide reaches for a marker buoy,
The wide channel for a patch of oil,
The hours tick on and men do not look at one
   another:
The divers sit beside their helmets,
The seahawks circle and make no sign,
The telephonists are mute;
And she lies: somewhere on this sloping shelf of
   Europe,
Thirty to fifty fathoms down and a fathom is six
   foot;
Here on this reef that slopes to the awful plunge
   beyond Rockall,
Hugged in the sands of the seabed,
Spiked on a raging rock tooth,
A hulk, a shell to be located,
With seventy-five crew all told, officers and ratings;
And the second day was like eternity,
Like a terrible evening that would never end—
   (Oh, let it end for them, let it end)
But on the third day landward the air was sweet,
The searchers looked and saw the white cliffs, the
   shoreline,
And remembered their homes and wives.

Whatever agony had been was over;
For seventy-five volunteers, seventy-five reasons
   for volunteering,
It was over; let no one say it was quick, it was easy:
Poor lads lost in the ground are not so lost as these!
Was it not quicker, easier, to have died in simple
   shipwreck?

Hurled unmannerly on the rocks, smashed by the
  white wind,
Rolled over with the gravel pounding into eyes and
  ears,
There would have been time for the last thoughts,
Time to expand the bursting lungs for the last time,
Time for the last look at the lost sky and the lost
  stars.
Time to make your soul, and return it
Whither you will, and either way to a stone Father's
  keeping!
It is a good death, shipwreck, compared to some
  deaths.
But this is not it, it is not this at all:
For so they might have died, begging the question
  that remains.

In this ship, in this one-purpose hull of death,
Was enacted this scarcely imaginable trapped
  horror
Before which the mind fails, where the spirit cannot
  enter.
Miners, politicals, poor people, sick, have been
  buried alive,
Coffined in earth alive, trodden down,
And yet their death seems not so terrible as this!
The terror of water is greater than any other terror,
Greater than the terror of fire, of tempest, of falling:
Let sun, moon, stars blaze out in a cataract of
  darkness
And there is grandeur, there is man mightier than
  the atom;
But here is deathly quiet, here is slow drift and
  soundless bell,
Here is enfolding and pressure, crushing of an
  eggshell.

There were coffinships once that were freedom itself
  to this ship,
Slave ships that offered a choice of deaths:
And this so vulnerable thing,
This puny thing was man's shark of the deep, at
  whose snap
Great liners might shake and quiver, bleed with a
  mortal wound!
In this steel belly were men and men, sons and
  brothers,
Men, trained to strike and kill. They are mourned
  now
But wives and mothers with bitter mouths
Are not bitter to speak against that purpose
For which their men have dived and surfaced,
Surfaced and dived, practised to make perfect and
Until the newsboys shouted War.

Why did we shed our gills and fins?
Why did we rise from our protozoic bed, sea-slime
  and ooze?
Bones that no coral make,
Eye sockets without eyes, without pearls,
Skulls and iron entrails, bones crossed over bones!
For these, the sea will not give birth,
To these, the harvest home will never come,
Nor the seagold anemone hoist sail for the western
  isles!

Is it to find the fault alone we would recover them?
The gauge or valve that perplexingly refused to
  work,
The pressure door that pressure did not withstand,
Even the dread acidic gas and death, after all, in the
  instant?
Rather let the heat break, stone Father!

If recovering is but to perfect the killer's perfection,
Nothing of purpose altered; nothing in us changed:
Then let the heart break, let the oceans invade and
    cover,
Let the cities and seaports be covered,
The great bulls of Antarctica roar on Snowdonia and
    the Pennines,
And man and his destiny cease.

*   *   *

Look, her replacement glides down the Tyneyard
    slipway,
And H.M. Submarine Affray the Second takes the
    tide:
Do not clap or cheer. Be silent, the land is silent.
Silence over all: to the slow bell, to the mournful
    whistle,
Past the dim wharves, as she swings to the river,
To the tide, to her first anchorage, first action
    stations.
Here is Death on a voyage of death, and could have
    been
H.M. Discovery or Beagle, Beagle the Second,
Bound for the coral mountains and wavy
    plantations deep!
Silent and sinister, let her go in silence.
Until destruction sickens of destruction, sickens and
    dies,
Listen only to the bell, listen and repeat:
"This is the ship that takes our sons, our lovers,
And returns them from whence they came,"
Over and over:
That the child may learn, in time, in time.

Ewart Milne

✤ Ballad

O! shairly ye hae seen my love
Doun whaur the waters wind:
He walks like ane wha fears nae man
And yet his e'en are kind.

O! shairly ye hae seen my love
At the turnin o' the tide;
For then he gethers in the nets
Doun be the waterside.

O! lassie I hae seen your love
At the turnin o' the tide;
And he was wi' the fisher-folk
Doun be the waterside.

The fisher-folk were at their trade
No far frae walnut grove;
They gethered in their dreepin nets
And fund your ain true love.

William Soutar

Fair Helen of Kirkconnell

I wish I were where Helen lies,
Night and day on me she cries,
O that I were where Helen lies,
   On fair Kirkconnell Lee!

Curst be the heart that thought the thought
And curst the hand that fired the shot,
When in my arms burd* Helen dropt,
   And died to succour me.

* girl

O think na but my heart was sair,
When my love dropt down and spak nae mair,
There did she swoon wi' meikle care,
    On fair Kirkconnell Lee.

As I went down the water side,
None but my foe to be my guide,
None but my foe to be my guide
    On fair Kirkconnell Lee;

I lighted down, my sword did draw,
I hacked him in pieces sma',
I hacked him in pieces sma',
    For her sake that died for me.

O Helen fair, beyond compare,
I'll make a garland of thy hair,
Shall bind my heart for evermair,
    Until the day I die.

O that I were where Helen lies!
Day and night on me she cries;
Out of my bed she bids me rise,
    Says, "Haste and come to me!"

O Helen fair, O Helen chaste!
If I were with thee I were blest,
Where thou liest low and tak'st thy rest
    On fair Kirkconnell Lee.

I wish my grave were growing green,
A winding-sheet drawn ower my een,
And I in Helen's arms lying,
    On fair Kirkconnell Lee.

I wish I were where Helen lies,
Night and day on me she cries,
For I am weary of the skies,
    For her sake that died for me.

Anonymous

✤ A Trampwoman's Tragedy

From Wynyard's Gap the livelong day
The livelong day,
We beat afoot the northward way
We had travelled times before.
The sun-blaze burning on our backs,
Our shoulders sticking to our packs,
By fosseway, fields, and turnpike tracks
We skirted sad Sedge-Moor.

Full twenty miles we jaunted on,
We jaunted on,—
My fancy-man, and jeering John,
And Mother Lee, and I.
And, as the sun drew down to west,
We climbed the toilsome Poldon crest,
And saw, of landskip sights the best,
The inn that beamed thereby.

For months we had padded side by side,
Ay, side by side
Through the Great Forest, Blackmoor wide,
And where the Parret ran.
We'd faced the gusts on Mendip ridge,
Had crossed the Yeo unhelped by bridge,
Been stung by every Marshwood midge,
I and my fancy-man.

Lone inns we loved, my man and I,
My man and I;
"King's Stag", "Windwhistle" high and dry.
"The Horse" on Hintock Green.
The cosy house at Wynyard's Gap,
"The Hut" renowned on Bredy Knap,
And many another wayside tap
Where folk might sit unseen.

Now as we trudged—O deadly day,
O deadly day!—
I teased my fancy man in play
And wanton idleness.
I walked alongside jeering John,
I laid his hand my waist upon;
I would not bend my glance on
My lover's dark distress.

Thus Poldon top at last we won,
At last we won,
And gained the inn at sink of sun
Far-famed as "Marshal's Elm".
Beneath us figured tor and lea,
From Mendip to the western sea—
I doubt if finer sight there be
Within this royal realm.

Inside the settle all a-row—
All four a-row
We sat, I next to John, to show
That he had wooed and won.
And then he took me on his knee,
And swore it was his turn to be
My favoured mate, and Mother Lee
Passed to my former one.

Then in a voice I had never heard,
I had never heard,
My only Love to me: "One word
My lady, if you please!
Whose is the child you are like to bear?—
His? After all my months o' care?"
God knows 'twas not! But, O despair!
I nodded—still to tease.

Then up he sprung, and with his knife—
And with his knife
He let out jeering Johnny's life,
Yes; there, at set of sun.
The slant ray through the window nigh
Gilded John's blood and glazing eye,
Ere scarcely Mother Lee and I
Knew that the deed was done.

The taverns tell the gloomy tale,
The gloomy tale,
How that at Ivel-chester jail
My Love, my sweetheart swung;
Though stained till now by no misdeed
Save one horse ta'en in time o' need;
(Blue Jimmy stole right many a steed
Ere his last fling he flung.)

Thereaft I walked the world alone,
Alone, alone!
On his death-day I gave my groan
And dropt his dead-born child.
'Twas nigh the jail, beneath a tree,
None tending me; for Mother Lee
Had died at Glaston, leaving me
Unfriended on the wild.

And in the night as I lay weak,
As I lay weak,
The leaves a-falling on my cheek,
The red moon low declined—
The ghost of him I'd die to kiss
Rose up and said: "Ah, tell me this!
Was the child mine, or was it his?
Speak, that I rest may find!"

O doubt not but I told him then,
I told him then,
That I had kept me from all men
Since we joined lips and swore.
Whereat he smiled, and thinned away
As the wind stirred to call up day . . .
—'Tis past! And here alone I stray
Haunting the Western Moor.

Thomas Hardy

The Haystack in the Floods

Had she come all the way for this,
To part at last without a kiss?
Yea, had she borne the dirt and rain
That her own eyes might see him slain
Beside the haystack in the floods?

Along the dripping leafless woods,
The stirrup touching either shoe,
She rode astride as troopers do;
With kirtle kilted to her knee,
To which the mud splashed wretchedly;
And the wet dripped from every tree

Upon her head and heavy hair,
And on her eyelids broad and fair;
And tears and rain ran down her face.
By fits and starts they rode apace,
And very often was his place
Far off from her; he had to ride
Ahead, to see what might betide
When the roads crossed; and sometimes, when
There rose a murmuring from his men,
Had to turn back with promises;
Ah me; she had but little ease;
And often for pure doubt and dread
She sobbed, made giddy in the head
By the swift riding; while, for cold,
Her slender fingers scarce could hold
The wet reins; yea, and scarcely, too,
She felt the foot within her shoe
Against the stirrup: all for this.
To part at last without a kiss
Beside the haystack in the floods.

For when they neared that old soaked hay,
They saw across the only way
That Judas, Codmar, and the three
Red running lions dismally
Grinned from his pennon, under which
In one straight line along the ditch,
They counted thirty heads.
                              So then,
While Robert turned round to his men,
She saw at once the wretched end,
And, stooping down, tried hard to rend
Her coif the wrong way from her head,
And hid her eyes; while Robert said:
"Nay, love, 'tis scarcely two to one,
At Poictiers where we made them run

So fast—why, sweet my love, good cheer,
The Gascon frontier is so near,
Nought after this."

*   *   *

But, "O", she said,
"My God; my God! I have to tread
The long way back without you; then
The court at Paris; those six men;
The gratings of the Chatelet;
The swift Seine on some rainy day
Like this, and people standing by,
And laughing, while my weak hands try
To recollect how strong men swim.
All this, or else a life with him,
For which I should be damned at last.
Would God that this next hour were past!"

He answered not, but cried his cry,
"St. George for Marny!" cheerily;
And laid his hand upon her rein.
Alas! no man of all his train
Gave back that cheery cry again;
And, while for rage his thumb beat fast
Upon his sword-hilt, some one cast
About his neck a kerchief long,
And bound him.

Then they went along
To Godmar; who said: "Now, Jehane,
Your lover's life is on the wane
So fast, that, if this very hour
You yield not as my paramour,
He will not see the rain leave off—
Nay, keep your tongue from gibe and scoff,
Sir Robert, or I slay you now."

She laid her hand upon her brow,
Then gazed upon the palm, as though
She thought her forehead bled, and—"No"
She said, and turned her head away,
As there were nothing else to say,
And everything were settled; red
Grew Godmar's face from chin to head:
"Jehane, on yonder hill there stands
My castle, guarding well my lands;
What hinders me from taking you,
And doing that I list to do
To your fair wilful body, while
Your knight lies dead?"

A wicked smile
Wrinkled her face, her lips grew thin,
A long way out she thrust her chin:
"You know that I should strangle you
While you were sleeping; or bite through
Your throat, by God's help: ah!" she said
"Lord Jesus, pity your poor maid!
For in such wise they hem me in,
I cannot choose but sin and sin,
Whatever happens; yet I think
They could not make me eat or drink,
And so should I just reach my rest."

"Nay, if you do not my behest,
O Jehane! though I love you well",
Said Godmar, "would I fail to tell
All that I know?" "Foul lies," she said.
"Eh? lies, my Jehane? by God's head,
At Paris folks would deem them true!
Do you know, Jehane, they cry for you,
'Jehane the brown! Jehane the brown!
Give us Jehane to burn or drown!'

Eh—gag me Robert!—sweet my friend,
This were indeed a piteous end
For those long fingers, and long feet,
And long neck, and smooth shoulders sweet;
An end that few men would forget
That saw it. So, an hour yet:
Consider, Jehane, which to take
Of life or death!"

               So, scarce awake,
Dismounting, did she leave that place,
And totter some yards: with her face
Turned upward to the sky she lay,
Her head on a wet heap of hay,
And fell asleep: and while she slept,
And did not dream, the minutes crept
Round to the twelve again; but she,
Being waked at last, sighed quietly,
And strangely childlike came, and said:
"I will not." Straightway Godmar's head,
As though it hung on strong wires, turned
Most sharply round, and his face burned.

For Robert—both his eyes were dry,
He could not weep, but gloomily
He seemed to watch the rain; yea, too,
His lips were firm; he tried once more
To touch her lips; she reached out, sore
And vain desire so tortured them,
The poor grey lips, and now the hem
Of his sleeve brushed them.
               With a start
Up Godmar rose, thrust them apart;
From Robert's throat he loosed the bands
Of silk and mail; with empty hands

Held out, she stood and gazed, and saw,
The long bright blade without a flaw
Glide out from Godmar's sheath, his hand
In Robert's hair; she saw him bend
Back Robert's head; she saw him send
The thin steel down; the blow told well,
Right backward the knight Robert fell,
And moaned as dogs do, being half dead,
Unwitting, as I deem: so then
Godmar turned grinning to his men,
Who ran, some five or six, and beat
His head to pieces at their feet,

Then Godmar turned again and said:
"So, Jehane, the first fitte* is read!
Take note, my lady, that your way
Lies backward to the Chatelet!"
She shook her head and gazed awhile
At her cold hands with a rueful smile,
As though this thing had made her mad.

This was the parting that they had
Beside the haystack in the floods.

William Morris

✤ Emperors of the Island

There is the story of a deserted island
where five men walked down to the bay.

The story of this island is
that three men would two men slay.

* canto

124

Three men dug two graves in the sand,
three men stood on the sea wet rock,
three shadows moved away.

There is the story of a deserted island
where three men walked down to the bay.

The story of this island is
that two men would one man slay.

Two men dug one grave in the sand,
two men stood on the sea wet rock,
two shadows moved away.

There is the story of a deserted island
where two men walked down to the bay.

The story of this island is
that one man would one man slay.

One man dug one grave in the sand,
one man stood on the sea wet rock,
one shadow moved away.

There is the story of a deserted island
where four ghosts walked down to the bay.

The story of this island is
that four ghosts would one man slay.

Four ghosts dug one grave in the sand,
four ghosts stood on the sea wet rock;
five ghosts moved away.

Dannie Abse

Parable

Two neighbours, who were rather dense,
Consider that their mutual fence
Were more symbolic of their peace
(Which they maintained should never cease)
If each about his home and garden
Set up a more substantial warden.
Quickly they cleared away the fence
To build a wall at great expense;
And soon their little plots of ground
Were barricaded all around:
Yet still they added stone to stone,
As if they never would be done,
For when one neighbour seemed to tire
The other shouted: Higher! Higher!
Thus day by day, in their unease,
They built the battlements of peace
Whose shadows, like a gathering blot,
Darkened on each neglected plot,
Until the ground, so overcast,
Became a rank and weedy waste.

Now in obsession, they uprear;
Jealous, and proud, and full of fear:
And, lest they halt for lack of stone,
They pull their dwelling-houses down.
At last, by their insane excess,
Their ramparts guard a wilderness;
And hate, arousing out of shame,
Flares up into a wondrous flame:
They curse; they strike; they break the wall
Which buries them beneath its fall.

William Soutar

The Dong with a Luminous Nose

When awful darkness and silence reign
Over the great Gromboolian plain,
Through the long, long wintry nights;—
When the angry breakers roar
As they beat on the rocky shore;—
When Storm-clouds brood on the towering heights
Of the Hills of the Chankly Bore:—
Then, through the vast and gloomy dark,
There moves what seems a fiery spark,
A lonely spark with silvery rays
Piercing the coal-black night,—
A meteor strange and bright:—
Hither and thither the vision strays,
A single lurid light.

Slowly it wanders,—pauses,—creeps,—
Anon it sparkles,—flashes and leaps;
And ever as onward it gleaming goes
A light on the Bong-tree stems it throws.
And those who watch at that midnight hour
From Hall, or Terrace or lofty Tower,
Cry, as the wild light passes along,—
    "The Dong!—the Dong!
    The wandering Dong through the forest goes!
    The Dong! the Dong!
    The Dong with a luminous Nose!"

Long years ago
The Dong was happy and gay,
Till he fell in love with a Jumbly Girl
Who came to those shores one day.
For the Jumblies came in a Sieve, they did,—
Landing at eve near the Zemmery Fidd

Where the Oblong Oysters grow,
And the rocks are smooth and gray.
And all the woods and the valleys rang
With the Chorus they daily and nightly sang,—
  "Far and few, far and few,
  Are the lands where the Jumblies live;
  Their heads are green, and their hands are blue,
  And they went to sea in a Sieve."

Happily, happily passed those days!
While the cheerful Jumblies staid;
They danced in circlets all night long,
To the plaintive pipe of the lively Dong,
In moonlight, shine, or shade.
For day and night he was always there
By the side of the Jumbly Girl so fair,
With her sky-blue hands, and her sea-green hair,
Till the morning came of that hateful day
When the Jumblies sailed in their Sieve away,
And the Dong was left on the cruel shore
Gazing—gazing for evermore,—
Ever keeping his weary eyes on
That pea-green sail on the far horizon,—
Singing the Jumbly Chorus still
As he sat all day on the grassy hill,—
  "Far and few, far and few,
  Are the lands where the Jumblies live;
  Their heads are green, and their hands are blue,
  And they went to sea in a Sieve."

But when the sun was low in the West,
The Dong arose and said,—
"What little sense I once possessed
Has quite gone out of my head!"
And since that day he wanders still

By lake and forest, marsh and hill,
Singing—"O somewhere, in valley or plain
Might I find my Jumbly Girl again!
For ever I'll seek by lake and shore
Till I find my Jumbly Girl once more!"
Playing a pipe with silvery squeaks,
Since then his Jumbly Girl he seeks,
And because by night he could not see,
He gathered the bark of the Twangum Tree
On the flowery plain that grows.
And he wove him a wondrous Nose,—
A Nose as strange as a Nose could be!
Of vast proportions and painted red,
And tied with cords to the back of his head.
—In a hollow rounded space it ended
With a luminous lamp within suspended,
All fenced about
With a bandage stout
To prevent the wind from blowing it out;—
And with holes all round to send the light,
In gleaming rays on the dismal night.
And now each night, and all night long,
Over those plains still roams the Dong;
And above the wail of the Chimp and Snipe
You may hear the squeak of his plaintive pipe
While ever he seeks, but seeks in vain,
To meet with his Jumbly Girl again;
Lonely and wild—all night he goes,—
The Dong with a luminous Nose!
And all who watch at the midnight hour,
From Hall, or Terrace, or lofty Tower,
Cry, as they trace the Meteor bright,
Moving along through the dreary night,—
    "This is the hour when forth he goes,
    The Dong with a luminous Nose!
    Yonder—over the plain he goes;

He goes!
He goes;
The Dong with a luminous Nose!"

Edward Lear

The Hunchback in the Park

The hunchback in the park
A solitary mister
Propped between trees and water
From the opening of the garden lock
That lets the trees and water enter
Until the Sunday sombre bell at dark

Eating bread from a newspaper
Drinking water from the chained cup
That the children filled with gravel
In the fountain basin where I sailed my ship
Slept at night in a dog kennel
But nobody chained him up.

Like the park birds he came early
Like the water he sat down
And Mister they called Hey mister
The truant boys from the town
Running when he had heard them clearly
On out of sound

Past lake and rockery
Laughing when he shook his paper
Hunchbacked in mockery
Through the loud zoo of the willow groves
Dodging the park keeper
With his stick that picked up leaves.

And the old dog sleeper
Alone between nurses and swans
While the boys among willows
Made the tigers jump out of their eyes
To roar on the rockery stones
And the groves were blue with sailors

Made all the day until bell time
A woman figure without fault
Straight as a young elm
Straight and tall from his crooked bones
That she might stand in the night
After the locks and chains

All night in the unmade park
After the railings and shrubberies
The birds the grass the trees the lake
And the wild boys innocent as strawberries
Had followed the hunchback
To his kennel in the dark.

Dylan Thomas

❋ Cap and Bells

The jester walked in the garden:
The garden had fallen still;
He bade his soul rise upward
And stand on her window-sill.

It rose in a straight blue garment,
When owls began to call;
It had grown wise-tongued by thinking
Of a quiet and light footfall;

But the young queen would not listen;
She rose in her pale night gown;
She drew in the heavy casement
And pushed the latches down.

He bade his heart go to her,
When the owls called out no more;
In a red and quivering garment
It sang to her through the door.

It had grown sweet-tongued by dreaming
Of a flutter of flower-like hair,
But she took up her fan from the table
And waved it off the air.

"I have cap and bells," he pondered,
"I will send them to her and die";
And when the morning whitened
He left them where she went by.

She laid them upon her bosom,
Under a cloud of her hair,
And her red lips sang them a love song;
Till stars grew out of the air.

She opened her door and her window,
And the heart and the soul came through,
To her right hand came the red one,
To her left hand came the blue.

They set up a noise like crickets,
A chattering wise and sweet,
And her hair was a folded flower
And the quiet of love in her feet.

William Butler Yeats

Kubla Khan

In Xanadu did Kubla Khan
A stately pleasure-dome decree:
Where Alph, the sacred river, ran
Through caverns measureless to man
  Down to a sunless sea.
So twice five miles of fertile ground
With walls and towers were girdled round:
And there were gardens bright with sinuous rills,
Where blossomed many an incense-bearing tree;
And here were forests ancient as the hills,
Enfolding sunny spots of greenery.

But oh! that deep romantic chasm which slanted
Down the green hill athwart a cedarn cover!
A savage place! as holy and enchanted
As e'er beneath a waning moon was haunted
By woman wailing for her demon-lover!
And from this chasm, with ceaseless turmoil seething,
As if this earth in fast thick pants were breathing,
A mighty fountain momently was forced:
Amid whose swift half-intermitted burst
Huge fragments vaulted like rebounding hail,
Or chaffy grain beneath the thresher's flail:
And 'mid these dancing rocks at once and ever
It flung up momently the sacred river.
Five miles meandering with a mazy motion
Through wood and dale the sacred river ran,
Then reached the caverns measureless to man,
And sank in tumult to a lifeless ocean:
And 'mid this tumult Kubla heard from far
Ancestral voices prophesying war!
  The shadow of the dome of pleasure
  Floated midway on the waves;

Where was heard the mingled measure
From the fountain and the caves.
It was a miracle of rare device,
A sunny pleasure-dome with caves of ice!

A damsel with a dulcimer
In a vision once I saw:
It was an Abyssinian maid,
And on her dulcimer she played,
Singing of Mount Abora.
Could I revive within me
Her symphony and song,
To such a deep delight 'twould win me,
That with music loud and long,
I would build that dome in air,
That sunny dome! those caves of ice!
And all who heard should see them there,
And all should cry, Beware! Beware!
His flashing eyes, his floating hair!
Weave a circle round him thrice,
And close your eyes with holy dread,
For he on honey-dew hath fed,
And drunk the milk of Paradise.

S. T. Coleridge

A Person from Porlock

There came a knocking at the front door,
The eternal, nameless caller at the door;
The sound pierced the still hall,
But not the stillness about his brain.
It came again. He arose, pacing the floor
Strewn with books, his mind big with the poem
Soon to be born, his nerves tense to endure
The long torture of delayed birth.

Delayed birth: the embryo maimed in the womb
By the casual caller, the chance cipher that jogs
The poet's elbow, spilling the cupped dream.

The encounter over, he came, seeking his room;
Seeking the contact with his lost self;
Groping his way endlessly back
On the poem's path, calling by name
The foetus stifling in the mind's gloom.

R. S. Thomas

❊ The Last Hour

Faust. Ah, Faustus.
   Now hast thou but one bare hour to live,
   And then thou must be damn'd perpetually!
   Stand still, you ever-moving spheres of heaven,
   That time may cease, and midnight never come;
   Fair Nature's eye, rise, rise again, and make
   Perpetual day; or let this hour be but
   A year, a month, a week, a natural day,
   That Faustus may repent and save his soul!
   O lente, lente currite, noctis equi!
   The stars move still, time runs, the clock will
      strike,
   The devil will come, and Faustus must be damn'd.
   O, I'll leap up to my God!—Who pulls me down?—
   See, see, where Christ's blood streams in the
      firmament!
   One drop would save my soul, half a drop: ah,
      my Christ!—
   Ah, rend not my heart for naming of my Christ!
   Yet will I call on him: O, spare me, Lucifer!—
   Where is it now? 'tis gone: and see, where God
   Stretcheth out his arm, and bends his ireful brows!

Mountains and hills, come, come, and fall on me,
And hide me from the heavy wrath of God!
No, no!
Then will I headlong run into the earth:
Earth, gape! O, no, it will not harbour me!
You stars that reign'd at my nativity,
Whose influence hath allotted death and hell,
Now draw up Faustus, like a foggy mist,
Into the entrails of yon labouring clouds,
That, when you vomit forth into the air,
My limbs may issue from your smoky mouths,
So that my soul may ascend to heaven!
(The clock strikes the half-hour.
Ah, half the hour is past! 'twill all be past anon.
O God,
If thou wilt not have mercy on my soul,
Yet for Christ's sake, whose blood hath ransom'd me,
Impose some end to my incessant pain;
Let Faustus live in hell a thousand years,
A hundred thousand, and at last be sav'd!
O, no end is limited to damned souls!
Why wert thou not a creature wanting soul?
Or why is this immortal that thou hast?
Ah, Pythagoras' metempsychosis, were that true,
This soul should fly from me, and I be chang'd
Unto some brutish beast! All beasts are happy,
For, when they die,
Their souls are soon dissolv'd in elements;
But mine must live still to be plagu'd in hell.
Curs'd be the parents that engender'd me!
No, Faustus, curse thyself, curse Lucifer
That hath depriv'd thee of the joys of heaven.
(The clock strikes twelve.
O, it strikes, it strikes! Now, body, turn to air,
Or Lucifer will bear thee quick to hell!
(Thunder and lightning.

O soul, be chang'd into little water-drops,
And fall into the ocean, ne'er be found!
Enter Devils
My God, my God, look not so fierce on me!
Adders and serpents, let me breathe a while!
Ugly hell, gape not! come not, Lucifer!
I'll burn my books!—Ah, Mephistophilis!

Christopher Marlowe
from "Dr Faustus"

Death and General Putnam

His iron arm had spent its force,
No longer might he rein a horse;
Lone, beside the dying blaze,
Dreaming dreams of other days,
    Sat old Israel Putnam.

Twice he heard, then three times more,
A knock upon the oaken door,
A knock he could not fail to know,
That old man in the ember glow.
    "Come," said Israel Putnam.

The door swung wide; in cloak and hood,
Lean and tall the pilgrim stood
And spoke in tones none else might hear,
"Once more I come to bring you fear!"
    "Fear!" said General Putnam.

"You know not fear? and yet this face
Your eyes have seen in many a place
Since first in stony Pomfert, when
You dragged the mad wolf from her den."
    "Yes," said General Putnam.

"Was I not close, when, stripped and bound,
With blazing faggots heaped around,
You heard the Huron war cry shrill?
Was I not close to Bunker Hill?"
  "Close," said General Putnam.

"Am I not that which strong men dread
On stricken field or fevered bed,
On gloomy trail and stormy sea,
And dare you name my name to me?"
  "Death," said General Putnam.

"We have been comrades, you and I,
In chase and war beaneath this sky;
And now, whatever Fate may send,
Old comrade, can you call me friend?"
  "Friend!" said General Putnam.

Then up he rose, and forth they went,
Away from battleground, fortress, tent,
Mountain, wilderness, field and farm,
Death and the General, arm in arm,
  Death and General Putnam.

Arthur Guiterman

❋ The Italian in England

That second time they hunted me
From hill to plain, from shore to sea,
And Austria, hounding far and wide
Her bloodhounds thro' the country-side,
Breathed hot and instant on my trace,—
I made six days a hiding-place
Of that dry green old aqueduct
Where I and Charles, when boys, have plucked

The fire-flies from the roof above,
Bright creeping thro' the moss they love.
—How long it seems since Charles was lost!
Six days the soldiers crossed and crossed
The country in my very sight;
And when the peril ceased at night,
The sky broke out in red dismay
With signal-fires; well, there I lay
Close covered o'er in my recess,
Up to the neck in ferns and cress,
Thinking on Metternich our friend,
And Charles's miserable end,
And much beside, two days; the third,
Hunger o'ercame me when I heard
The peasants from the village go
To work among the maize; you know,
With us, in Lombardy, they bring
Provisions packed on mules, a string
With little bells that cheer their task,
And casks, and boughs on every cask
To keep the sun's heat from the wine;
These I let pass in jingling line,
And, close on them, dear noisy crew,
The peasants from the village, too;
And at the very rear would troop
Their wives and sisters in a group
To help, I knew; when these had passed,
I threw my glove to strike the last,
Taking the chance; she did not start,
Much less cry out, but stooped apart
One instant, rapidly glanced round,
And saw me beckon from the ground:
A wild bush grows and hides my crypt;
She picked my glove up while she stripped
A branch off, then rejoined the rest
With that; my glove lay in her breast:

Then I drew breath; they disappeared:
It was for Italy I feared.

An hour, and she returned alone
Exactly where my glove was thrown.
Meanwhile came many thoughts; on me
Rested the hopes of Italy;
I had devised a certain tale
Which, when 'twas told her, could not fail
Persuade a peasant of its truth;
I meant to call a freak of youth
This hiding, and give hopes of pay,
And no temptation to betray.
But when I saw that woman's face,
Its calm simplicity of grace,
Our Italy's own attitude
In which she walked thus far, and stood,
Planting each naked foot so firm,
To crush the snake and spare the worm—
At first sight of her eyes, I said,
"I am that man upon whose head
They fix the price, because I hate
The Austrians over us: the State
Will give you gold—oh, gold so much—
If you betray me to their clutch,
And be your death, for aught I know,
If once they find you saved their foe.
Now, you must bring me food and drink
And also paper, pen, and ink,
And carry safe what I shall write
To Padua, which you'll reach at night
Before the Duomo shuts; go in,
And wait till Tenebrae begin;
Walk to the third Confessional,
Between the pillar and the wall,
And kneeling whisper, *Whence comes peace?*

Say it a second time; then cease;
And if the voice inside returns,
From Christ and Freedom; what concerns
The cause of peace?—for answer, slip
My letter where you placed your lip;
Then come back happy we have done
Our mother service—I, the son,
As you the daughter of our land!"

Three mornings more, she took her stand
In the same place, with the same eyes:
I was no surer of sunrise
Than of her coming. We conferred
Of her own prospects, and I heard
She had a lover—stout and tall,
She said—then let her eyelids fall,
"He could do much"—as if some doubt
Entered her heart,—then, passing out,
"She could not speak for others—who
Had other thoughts; herself she knew":
And so she brought me drink and food.
After four days, the scouts pursued
Another path; at last arrived
The help my Paduan friends contrived
To furnish me: she brought the news.
For the first time I could not choose
But kiss her hand and lay my own
Upon her head—"This faith was shown
To Italy, our mother;—she
Uses my hand and blesses thee!"
She followed down to the seashore;
I left and never saw her more.

How very long since I have thought
Concerning—much less wished for—aught
Beside the good of Italy

For which I live and mean to die!
I never was in love; and since
Charles proved false, what shall now convince
My inmost heart I have a friend?
However, if I pleased to spend
Real wishes on myself—say, three—
I know at least what one should be.
I would grasp Metternich until
I felt his red wet throat distil
In blood thro' these two hands. And next,
—Nor much for that am I perplexed—
Charles, perjured traitor, for his part,
Should die slow of a broken heart
Under his new employers. Last
—Ah, there, what should I wish? For fast
Do I grow old and out of strength.—
If I resolved to seek at length
My father's house again, how scared
They all would look, and unprepared!
My brothers live in Austria's pay
—Disowned me long ago, men say;
And all my early mates who used
To praise me so—perhaps induced
More than one early step of mine—
Are turning wise; while some opine
"Freedom grows licence", some suspect
"Haste breeds delay", and recollect
They always said, such premature
Beginnings never could endure!
So, with a sullen "All's for best",
The land seems settling to its rest.
I think, then, I should wish to stand
This evening in that dear, lost land,
Over the sea the thousand miles,
And know if yet that woman smiles
With the calm smile; some little farm

She lives in there, no doubt; what harm
If I sat on the door-side bench,
And, while her spindle made a trench
Fantastically in the dust,
Inquired of all her fortunes—just
Her children's ages and their names,
And what may be the husband's aims
For each of them. I'd talk this out,
And sit there, for an hour about,
Then kiss her hand once more, and lay
Mine on her head, and go my way.
So much for idle wishing—how
It steals the time! To business now!

Robert Browning

The Ballad of Culver's Hole

What feet are heard about these rocks
This highest tide of the year?
White spray of the equinox,
You chill the heart with fear.

Two boats close in from East and West
On a little boat that feels
The lucky weight of Culver
Gripping the stolen creels.

Is it the rope of Culver
Where the shag has the wit to dive,
Dragged through the shivering breakers,
That makes these rocks alive?

A great, round barrel
He has rolled up that grey beach.
Voices like claws are closing in,
Almost within reach.

In a moment he has vanished.
The gully's packed with dread.
Where is he hiding in the rocks,
The man they took for dead?

"Between this headland and that point
He surely ran aground.
Who saw the cunning hare stop dead
To cheat the flying hound?

You up there, on the cliff's dark brows,
You who stand there stiff,
Where does Culver keep his house,
Perched upon what cliff?"

"We know nothing, we know nothing,
Never found his nest.
Ours is the crooked haystack,
The whitewashed farm at rest.

We hear nothing, we hear nothing,
Only seabirds' cries.
Call his name to the rock, and then
Hear what the rock replies.

A white-washed cottage, a house of stone
Might not hold your man.
Out of a nest of bleaching bone
The brightest fisher sprang.

We have seen the kestrel hang in the air
And where the ravens glide
Have combed the rocks for laver-bread
And the cockles in the tide.

But danger haunts the upper ledge
Here where the seagull flies.
Why do you ask gently
With murder in your eyes?

Watch, watch your footing.
The stones in the ledge are loose.
Under this hollow cliff the sea
Is hissing like a goose."

"Let two upon the green turf go
And two upon the rocks,
A great tide is running,
On the door of death it knocks.

It roars to have him hammered down
With nails to the sea bed.
Where is he hiding in the rocks,
The man we took for dead?"

"The equinox is rising;
The sky to the West is black,
The sea has drowned a hundred pools;
Should we not go back?"

"To think, that fish was in my net
And now has got away.
He beckons for the sun to set
And the waters fill the bay."

"Go back, go back, and leave him
Before it is too late.
The sea has drowned a thousand pools.
We cannot fight with Fate.

The great rock and the little rock,
They slip beneath the wave.
These breakers have drawn blood before,
Their lilies strewn a grave.

The mole beneath the giant sea
Is heaping mound on mound.
Make for the ship, come quickly,
Or we shall all be drowned."

"The dark is helping the digging mole
To cut our exit off.
Who could smoke out a smuggler's hole
In a sea so blind and rough?

God rot the guts of Culver
By whom the good man dies.
He laughs behind a wall of rock
Where every rock has eyes."

Now each rock wears disguises,
Each darkened stone deceives,
And louder the wave rises
With a noise of rustling leaves.

But before the long wave hit the ground
The shag had the wit to dive.
Those greyhounds covered at a bound
The hare they left alive.

Their noose is for the goose of the sea,
And they have not caught him yet,
A barrel rises slowly
Just where the sun had set.

                                        Vernon Watkins

Questions

The first two poems make a "protest". Each poet has gone about making his protest in an interesting and original way. Consider the method used by each poet. Which poem makes the greater impact on you?

"The Honourable Company" attempts to justify a way of thinking about which many people today would want to make a protest. A soldier is expected to do his duty. What happens to him if he refuses? Are there some orders that he would be justified in refusing to carry out?

What is the force of the word "naturally" (l. 4 and l. 20)? What is it that really disturbs the sharpshooter?

Has Blake's first statement more significance than the great complexity of little things that are revealed by a microscope? Can you think of moments which seemed to last for eternity? Were they always *bad* moments?

What is Blake's attitude to human cruelty to animals? Do you agree that small actions of cruelty may have such a destructive effect upon individual human beings and humanity itself?

Do you think this a justified comment on the way some children behave towards their pets?

A quality of poetry is that it says so much with comparatively few words. Is this true of this poem?

Show how by little details of observation the poet recreates for us this experience of his on a mountain road.

Was the action of the poet to the dead pregnant deer

the only possible one in the circumstances? Why does the poet describe his thinking "hard for us all" as his "only swerving"? Does the title have a double meaning?

Birds p. 6

What does the poet think is the essential difference between men and birds? What longing for a change does she express in the final stanza of the poem? Do you think birds are happier and better off than human beings? Can you think of any human qualities which although they may cause pain are of value?

A Dream of Horses p. 7
The Horses p. 9

What is there about horses and their relationship with man which have made them figure so frequently in poems and stories and myths?

Would you say that Ted Hughes' poem is concerned with the magic of horses, that he is using them as an image of divine or supernatural power?

How does the poet bring out the closeness of the grooms to the horses they look after? What effect does the phrase "mice in our pockets, straw in our hair" have on you?

Edwin Muir's poem tells of a remnant of mankind existing after "the seven days war". Consider the nature of the war. How does the poet bring about the sense of quiet and desolation after the catastrophe? What is the people's attitude to a civilization that has been destroyed?

How does the return of the horses mark the remaking of a link between man and the animal world? How and why had this link been broken?

The Man in the Bowler Hat p. 10
The Unknown Citizen p. 11
Jingle for Children p. 13

Would you say that all three poems are making a similar comment on a certain type of person? Do you think it is true and justified?

What is your explanation of the first line in verse 1 and the second line in verse 4 of "The Man in the Bowler Hat"?

In Auden's poem in what sense is the subject of the epitaph unknown? Would you agree that Auden's ironical treatment is particularly appropriate to his theme?

In "Jingle for Children" why has the poet italicized the first two lines of verse 3? Suggest how a merely passive and completely obedient attitude to life can be destructive.

Lollocks p. 13
Lollocks are creatures who mildly taunt the untidy, but they have a more unpleasant side to them. What do you understand by their being "nasty together" and by "dreams of vexation"? In what way does the charm at the end rescue the poem from the sinister turn it has taken?

In Praise of Herbs p. 15
Charms p. 16
These poems remind us of an earlier age when a less sophisticated people paid much more regard to the efficacy of herbs and the power of charms than we do today. Even so, to what extent do we still find superstition persisting in our society?

Spate in Winter Midnight p. 17
Contrast the behaviour of the adder with all other creatures during the storm and suggest why the poet calls the adder the "still centre" of the storm?

Do you think that "wild and shaking hair" gives a true picture of a mountain stream in flood?

Can you say why the poet says the fox shrinks through "Troys of bracken and Babel towers of rocks"? Remember that in a night of confused storm everything may appear larger than life and more menacing.

Inversnaid p. 17
Consider how Gerard Manley Hopkins blends words together, uses strange words, or invents new words to express the variety of wild nature?

From the last line point out what qualities of nature we may be in danger of destroying.

Ode to the West Wind p. 18

On one level Shelley's Ode tells about a real wind affecting real trees and real water. Can you point out what spiritual qualities of God or man the poem also celebrates? Can you think of other poems or stories which use fire and water in this same double way?

Point out some lines which express the poet's desire to become united to the onrushing wind? Do you think that a desire to be free from the petty restrictions and limitations of everyday life is part of the experience of most people?

Shelley was a revolutionary. Show how the last few lines of his Ode express his desire for a change and new birth both in man and society?

On the Balcony p. 21

A mood of love and tenderness is often associated with a landscape, weather or time of day. Consider this in the light of D. H. Lawrence's poem.

"What have we but each other?" What is implied by this question?

I know where I'm going p. 22

What contrast between love and marriage does this poem express? In some earlier versions of this song the last line puts "devil" instead of "dear". Which word do you consider more appropriate?

To his Love p. 22

Do you feel the language and rhythm of this sonnet is more dignified than that of the other poems? What difference does this make to your response to this poem?

Eternity p. 23

The difficulty of being in love is in keeping a certain independence without loving the other person the less.

One has also to believe in the other person's love and yet not try to make them surrender *their* independence.

An old pop song begins:

> "Stay sweet as you are,
> Don't ever change, dear."

Would this or the advice given by William Blake in "Eternity" be the better advice to build a good love relationship on?

If I were the Earth   p. 23

This poem tells of an attempt to achieve an almost complete oneness with another person. In the light of the final verse discuss whether or not the poet thinks this is possible.

O, My Luve is like a Red, Red Rose   p. 24

Why has the rose so often been used as a symbol or image of love?

The Sick Rose   p. 25

The "invisible worm" suggests an evil and unhealthy guilt. What effect does this guilt have on the rose of love? Can you think of instances of how such spoiling of love comes about?

As I walked out one Evening   p. 25

Do you think that the impossible situations described in verses 3 and 4 make the poet's protestation of love more sincere or less sincere? What effect does time have on his vows? Can you give a practical example of what he means when he writes

> "Time watches from the shadow
> And coughs when you would kiss."?

How (verse 11) does Auden manage to bring out the sadness and boredom of little happenings and situations? In verse 14 what is the significance of the adjective "crooked"? In the last line of the poem is the poet thinking of an actual river, or is it life itself he is thinking of?

Besides the theme of longing the first three poems have
something in common. They use very few words but with
a very few words express deep feeling. They are a kind of
trap for feeling. Try to add to them by description or
embellishment and you only detract from their poignancy.

The Tennyson poem gains much of its power from
contrasts. What are these contrasts and how do they
increase the sense of grief? Although it is a sad poem
would you say that its final effect is one of sadness?

A Poison Tree   p. 29

Show how by use of words and images Blake expresses
the hatred that can be much more evil and destructive
if we refuse to admit that it exists in ourselves.

A Case of Murder   p. 30

Do you think that a child might behave as cruelly as the
boy in this case of murder? Compare incidents in *Lord of
the Flies* by William Goulding.

What does the poet mean by the boy being unable to
hide from the swelling cupboard and the huge black cat?
Is he referring to a real cat or what will happen to the
boy's mind? Compare the story by Edgar Allan Poe:
The Black Cat.

Spain, 1809   p. 31

What was happening in Spain at this date? Do you agree
that the horror of the theme of this poem is made all the
more terrible by being left uncertain and indefinite?

> "I will not tell, under that white moonshine,
>   What things were done."

Can you expand on this?

What is the significance of the lines in brackets in the
last verse?

They that have Power to Hurt   p. 34

Like Blake's poem this also is about people who bottle up their feelings, but Shakespeare has in mind people who do this because their nature is cold and their feelings shallow. Does he really mean that such people "inherit Heaven's graces" or is he being ironic about a type of person he thoroughly dislikes?

Nationality   p. 35

What justification is there for including this poem with a group of "hate" poems?

Lucifer in Starlight   p. 35
Innocent's Song   p. 36

Here are two poems about wicked people. One is of Lucifer, the fallen angel of God, the other of King Herod who wished to destroy the infant Christ and tried to do so by killing all the children of Christ's age.

Remembering that he was once called the "Morning Star" and was a leader among God's angels, comment on Meredith's picture of Lucifer. Does Lucifer suggest the pettiness of much evil or a certain majesty?

Does Causley intend Herod to be a comic or a sinister figure?

Why does Herod wear rubies? Why does he *caw* his carol, and what makes the snow run red? Saffron buns, gingerbread, Christmas flame: when applied to Herod what effect do these aspects of the jollity and feasting of Christmas have on you?

Remember Herod's interview with the Magi and suggest why "double-talking" describes his behaviour.

Schoolmaster   p. 37
The French Master   p. 38

In both poems the teachers have undergone a similar and unpleasant experience? Show how the poets both hint at the experience but do not state it directly. Does this help us to see what has happened from the viewpoint of the members of the class? Compare the difference in treatment of the two teachers. Yevtushenko brings out the pathos of the old teacher. How does the snow falling on him bring out this sense of pity?

Consider the changes in the attitude of Walter Bird to his class and the consequent changes of the attitude of the class to Walter Bird.

Food for Powder p. 40
The quotations from Shakespeare which begin and end this section show through Falstaff that he could be cynical about war and understood its waste and futility.

A Square Dance p. 40
In *Goodbye to All That* Robert Graves describes how soldiers going up a trench would shake hands with the hand of a corpse embedded in the rampart; shake hands jokingly. When you find an experience almost intolerable you can sometimes escape from it by a savage joke. Consider these statements in relation to the rhythm and subject-matter of "A Square Dance".

Futility p. 41
Does this poem blame, or just state an incident of war? Remember that Owen wrote in the introduction to his poems—"My subject is war and the pity of it. The poetry is in the pity." Why does the poet call the sunbeams "fatuous"?

Attack p. 42
How does the description of the attack increase the force of the final punch-line "O Jesus, make it stop!"?

The Chances p. 42
Discuss the use of vernacular or everyday language in this poem. In what sense has Jim "All the lot"? What comment does this poem make about the outcome of war?

Grass p. 43

People have short memories of the tragedy of war. Is this what the poem is saying? Does it tell us anything about the outcome of war?

War Poet p. 44
Enfidaville p. 44
Parachutists p. 45

Three poems which each express a fresh and unusual view on the subject of war.

The War Poet finds himself making war when he had intended peace. How can this happen to a man? How in the last few lines does he manage to suggest the degradation and desolation that war brings?

"Enfidaville". Why are the images said to have fallen "like dancers"? Consider the effectiveness of the other similes in this poem. Does the presence of the ghosts make the scene more, or less, desolate? What prompts the poet to "love them at this minute"? What would "the blue eyes of the images" show?

"Parachutists". Are the parachutists any the less graceful and beautiful because they are the enemy?

The Soldier Addresses his Body p. 46
Roman Wall Blues p. 47

Do you find any similarity in attitude between the two soldiers to the war in which they are engaged? In the first poem what is the nature of the things the soldier would miss if he were killed?

How does Auden express the boredom and inanity of the soldier's life on the wall?

Aikichi Kuboyama p. 48
Your Attention Please p. 49
Bombs p. 51

Here are three poems all concerned with the capacity of human beings to destroy themselves and the world they live in.

The first poem is about an actual happening. The crew of the *Lucky Dragon* failed to pick up the warning message and all died, slowly, of the atomic dust which fell on their ship from the bomb which the Americans dropped—experimentally—somewhere in the Pacific. The poet, Zofia Ilinska, brings out both the innocence and the terrible fate of the crew. Is their tragedy emphasized by her reference to such ordinary details as their food, the tea they drank?

In "Your Attention Please" what is the intention of Peter Porter? What does he wish to bring home to us about the contrast between hydrogen bombs and the measures we are supposed to take against them?

"Bombs". My poem was touched off by one of the last lectures Robert Frost gave before he died. He said, "You know they're all talking about the Bomb and one of these days a bomb will sure go off, and a lot of people will go to the other side. D'you know what will happen then? Someone will say 'Boy, that sure was something!'" Since we all have to die why do we get so upset by untimely death?

The Convergence of the Twain p. 52
A Thought p. 53

Thomas Hardy suggests that our lives are determined by fate, by "the Spinner of the Years". Do you agree with this view?

Does Walt Whitman appear to side with Hardy? The last three lines of "A Thought" ask a question which is suggested in Hardy's poem. What is the question?

"Who's in the Next Room?" p. 54
Outside and In p. 55

These poems are made all the more sinister because we are not told who is in the next room or who is outside the house. Why is this so? Can you give examples from books, plays or films of such uncertainty creating terror? Is it true to say that once you have named and seen what you are frightened about it ceases to be frightening?

Here are three poems connected with old age. Do you think it best to avoid topics of this kind?

"Nineteenth Birthday". Mention some of the vivid observations of nature which make the poet's walk alive for us. Why is the village "lost" that the old woman wants the priest to tell her about? Suggest some reasons for the difficulty the priest has in conversing with her. What is the significance of the word "abyss"?

What difference in atmosphere and diction do you find between "When You are Old" and "An Old Woman's Lamentations"?

Some questions like that of James Stephens' philosopher can never be completely answered.

Tennyson was troubled by the conflict—it was particularly sharp in his day—which seemed to exist between religion and science. How could one reconcile a loving god with this often sad and cruel world? How could one reconcile divine care for the individual with the discoveries of evolution? Does this poem attempt to solve the conflict? Would it be a better poem if it did so?

This, appropriately, is almost the last poem that Tennyson wrote. In what way does the sea imagery assist the idea of a serene passing from life to death?

In the light of this strong and rhythmical statement about death consider the difference between poetry and prose.

A Form of Epitaph
p. 60
Consider the question and answer form of this poem. Beneath the dry, official language do you find any emotion?

No Coward Soul
p. 60
Emily Brontë was a mystic, that is to say someone who had immediate, personal experience of a realm of being not limited by time and space. Remembering this make a comparison of this poem with the others in the section.

In Memory of my Mother
p. 61
A Point of Honour
p. 62
Do not go gentle into that good night
p. 64
Portrait of a Stoic
p. 64
Although they are about death these poems are not predominantly sad. Can you determine why this is?

The final line in Kavanagh's poem says, "And you smile up at us". Do you feel some kind of dialogue can continue between the living and the dead if they understand each other, even if no words can be spoken?

When my mother was dying she seemed to be talking to her relations who had died before her. Do you agree with the sister who said she was "wandering", or do you think she was passing into a further world to meet people again who had died before her?

Dylan Thomas' angry poem is about the dying of his father. What statement does the poem make about death and about the attitude of his dying father towards death?

Explain the title "Portrait of a Stoic" and link up your answer with the last two lines of the poem. (Epictetus was a Greek Stoic philosopher who lived in the first century A.D.) What did the directors conclude from the outward behaviour of the bereaved husband? What were his real feelings? Show how they are brought home to us by small details of behaviour.

What Thomas said in a Pub
p. 65
Whether or not God is a "person", being people we have to think of him in a personal way. James Stephens de-

scribes a god far greater than any ordinary human being, but what personal and human characteristics does he give him?

Look up the story of Sodom and Gomorrah in the Bible. Is Stephens' poem saying something similar about the mercy of God?

God's Grandeur p. 66
Hopkins' language is difficult though rewarding. What do you think of the comparison "like shining from shook foil"?

What does Hopkins think men have done to this world?

I am the Great Sun p. 67
By building up image after image Causley shows the nearness of God to man. What comment does this poem make about man's attitude to God?

The Kingdom of God p. 67
Do you agree that Francis Thompson and Charles Causley are making similar comments about the nearness of God. But, why according to Thompson, does man often fail to find him?

Who is at my Window? p. 68
The stranger in this little poem, written about the year 1500, finds God no farther away than the other side of the window. What does he have to promise in order to enter the house?

From the Ballad of Reading Gaol p. 69
Wilde wrote the "Ballad of Reading Gaol", from which these verses are taken, while he was in prison. It is easy to see in which direction his own sympathies lay, but do you think a poem of this nature would have had power to win over opinion against capital punishment?

The Day Larry was Stretched p. 71

The poet is content merely to describe his surroundings
on the day. Is he successful in creating atmosphere? Which
in your opinion are the most effective images to match
this sombre event?

Day of these Days p. 72
Everyone Sang p. 73
Snatch of Sliphorn Jazz p. 73

Two poems of happy theme and a third offering a cautionary
note.

In "Day of these Days" what is it that has set alight
the poet's exultation? By what means does he invite the
reader to share his delight?

Siegfried Sassoon's war poems are mainly concerned
with the abomination and futility of war, but this poem
could not be more full of rapture and hope. What do you
think the occasion might have been that caused everyone
to burst out singing and why did it so touch the emotions
of the poet?

"Snatch of Sliphorn Jazz". Is this the language of
poetry? It is an amusing comment on life. Are we to take
it seriously?

Holiday Memory p. 74

Why does this piece lend itself to broadcasting? Does
the human voice add to its poetical quality? Does the
unusual use of language—a *fanfare* of sunshades, a *wince*
of bathers, a *lark* of boys—help us to see the scene in a
fresh way? Do you find the comparison of the boy with the
lion effective?

Dylan Thomas tells us that those "departed" summers
were always radiant and sky-blue. Do you think they
really were?

Trebetherick p. 75

This too is a poem expressing nostalgia for the days of
childhood, though here there is a hint in the darkness of

the wood of sinister shadows. What do you think the poet has in mind?

Robert Frost's language is the everyday speech of men and women. Do you agree with this? Does it make good poetry? How by referring to the ice he found on the drinking trough does he emphasize his extreme tiredness? In what way is it a troubled sleep that came to him and how does he manage to make the experiences he describes real?

The Shakespeare sonnet is concerned less with troubled sleep than with lying awake seeing not with the eyes but with the "soul's imaginary sight". In the passage from *The Tempest* Caliban touches upon the soothing power of music but he also makes an interesting observation on dreams. Can you suggest why he prefers dreams to reality?

Paul Dehn catches the sleeper at the point of waking. The minute-hand, the moon and the mind are said to "gather moment". Can you explain what is meant by this?

These poems each in a different way are expressing gratitude. Gratitude for what?

Hopkins has an unusual and original way of arranging his words, but even if some of the lines are difficult to understand it is easy to be carried along by his sense of gladness.

"Sunlight on the Garden" has a current of sadness. How do the rhyming words (notice how some of these fall at the *beginning* as well as at the end of the lines) add to the musical quality of the poem?

What do you think the poet's own answer would be to the question asked in the last line of "Shancoduff"?

Lord Randal p. 83

The old ballads dealt with simple passions, such as love and hate, which were readily understood by their audience. Is this true of "Lord Randal"?

The story is told in dialogue form. Do you think this method is successful? Try telling the story as for a newspaper, and compare the two accounts.

The refrain changes at the sixth verse. Think what the effect of this is. Which does Lord Randal find more difficult to bear: that he is dying or that he has been wronged by his "true love"?

Frankie and Johnnie p. 85

A traditional song from America. It is nearer to our own times than the ballads, but has it any reminders of them? What particular features does it share with "Lord Randal"?

Danny p. 87

Danny came to a violent end—probably well-deserved; but what is it that prevents this poem from becoming a tragedy in the same way as "Lord Randal" is a tragedy?

Farewell to Old England p. 88
The Greenwich Prisoner p. 89

The first of these is a "transportation" song. In the early part of the nineteenth century in England it was possible to be transported to Australia even for petty theft. What is the writer's attitude to his conviction? What would yours be in the same circumstances?

In what way can the sailor be said to be a prisoner in "The Greenwich Prisoner"? Does he show resentment?

The Castle p. 90
Two Wise Generals p. 92

The words "at ease" set the mood for the start of "The Castle". Which words of the poet particularly help to create the sense of security felt by the defenders? Why is there a pause after "and we were true . . ."? Think of the effect of the alliteration of the two lines which end the fourth verse.

Is there any way of guarding against treachery of this kind?

The story of black Douglas, here contrasted with the two generals, who gave his life defending the casket containing the heart of Robert the Bruce, is told in the poem "The Heart of the Bruce" by W. E. Aytoun.

How does the poet belittle the generals' medals? "Grab", "stuffed". Do these words help to reveal their character? Does the atmosphere of the later lines of the poem prepare us for the "twist" that comes at the very end? Is there any obvious explanation for the disaster that befell the generals? Does the uncertainty increase or lessen the force of the poem?

Although both these poems are about rather special and dramatic situations, could they refer to the lives of ordinary men and women? In other words do we also believe in a safe and secure way of life which in one moment may be shattered?

The High Tide on the Coast of Lincolnshire, 1571 p. 93

What effect did the tragedy have on the old woman? Is it her age alone that accounts for the unusual manner in which the story is related?

It is an event which, if it had happened today, would have made news headlines. What would a reporter miss out in telling the story, and would it be any the worse for the omissions?

Does the description of the eygre prepare the reader to hear of the death of Elizabeth and her children? What is particularly ironic about the bodies being found where they were?

The old woman mentioned different sounds she heard. What were they, and why did they carry so far?

A poem to compare: "The Sands of Dee" by Charles Kingsley.

The Death of Samson p. 98

Samson, after his blinding by the Philistines (Judges 16), has regained his strength and is forced to entertain his captors by giving displays of strength. In this passage from "Samson Agonistes" a messenger relates how Samson destroyed his enemies but at the same time brought about his own death. Why did Samson decide to take his own life? Does this account tell us anything interesting about the messenger himself?

The Orphan's Song p. 100
Death of a Bird p. 105

Consider why the bird died. Was it loss of freedom in each case?

Is there any parallel in Dobell's poem with "the bars of my hands"? In what way does the orphan identify himself with the bird? Dobell's language is of childlike simplicity—to match his orphan—but is the feeling any the less intense?

Silkin's poem is the angrier in tone. What is he really angry about? What is the "space" taken away from his mind? Do many people react in this way to this kind of situation?

The Burial of Sir John Moore p. 106

Sir John Moore, leader of the English army, was killed in the retreat before the French during the Peninsular War. He was buried hastily and without the full military honours due to him.

Would you agree that the poet has charged his account of the burial with genuine feeling? Are there any lines of special poignancy? Is the picture easy to *see*?

Elegy for a Lost Submarine p. 108

This poem with its haunting TAP TAP TAP TAP turns out to be much more than an elegy for *H.M.S. Affray*—and other submarines lost in peace and war. What do we learn about the searchers? How is death by other means made to seem preferable to death under the sea?

"Rather let the heart break, stone Father." Do you agree with this sentiment and the poet's suggestion of an unfeeling God?

"Until destruction sicken of destruction." Is this possible?

Two ballads telling of the death of a lover, the one gentle and restrained, the other passionate and angry. Listen to the music of the lines. Do you find it appropriate in each case to the feeling that the poet is creating?

The trampwoman was in love with her "fancy-man" and the life of freedom they lived. Why, when she was aware of his "dark distress", did she continue with her deception?

What is the special emphasis given by the repeated words which form the second line in each verse?

Although this is a complete poem, the poet gives us only the middle of the story. He relies upon the reader to supply the beginning and the end out of his imagination. What do you think is the story of Jehane, her lover, and Godmar before the poem opens?

"Jehane the brown! Jehane the brown!
Give us Jehane to burn or drown!"

What do these two lines tell us about the fate Jehane must meet if she is taken back to Paris? Of what would she be accused?

Each poem considers a darker side of man's nature, though in each case the treatment is different.

What has the man gained when the other four men have been killed? What has he lost?

Do the neighbours feel any more secure as their wall grows higher? Does this parable remind us of the way nations behave towards each other?

The Dong with a Luminous Nose
The Dong fell in love with a Jumbly girl. What effect did it have on him when she went away? Does this explain why he made himself a luminous nose and not just a lantern?

Despite some oddities and contradictions would you consider the Dong to be a real person and not just a nonsense creation?

This is a poem of distinct musical rhythms. Are there any lines you find particularly melodious?

The Hunchback in the Park
Like the Dong the hunchback dreams of a girl. Is it significant that she is " . . . without fault/Straight as a young elm."?

Do the boys seem real to you? Do they ever think of their cruelty when they mock the hunchback?

Cap and Bells
Kubla Khan
A Person from Porlock
"Cap and Bells" and "Kubla Khan" were each of them dreams written down in verse when their authors awoke. Yeats tells a complete tale though much of the detail is left to the imagination. "Kubla Khan" is unfinished, for Coleridge was disturbed by a caller ("a person from Porlock"), and when returning to his work he found that the image of his dream which once was so clear, had now faded.

"Cap and Bells" was a favourite poem of its author and one which he interpreted differently at different times.

What has happened to the merry-making of the jester? Having given his heart and his soul to the young queen, what has he left to give? Having received this gift, why is it only then—when it is too late—that she finds she loves the jester?

Rather than look for meaning in "Kubla Khan" it is better to consider the word pictures themselves. These are full of colour, sound and movement. Which colours come to mind? Which sounds? Which movement? Can you find examples of successful alliteration, and lines in which the sounds are specially suited to the sense?

"A Person from Porlock" is an interesting postscript to "Kubla Khan". What are the feelings implied by the words "the long torture of delayed birth"?

The Last Hour
Death and General Putnam

Marlowe lived at a time when men and women were starting to break away from the old dogmatic rules of the Church and explore both man and the world he lives in with a free-ranging intelligence. Marlowe himself professed to be an atheist.

Faustus has sold his soul to the devil, and here in the final lines from Marlowe's play is Faustus pleading with God for forgiveness. So impassioned is this magnificent language that it is difficult to disassociate the author from the character he has created. *Is* this Marlowe speaking? Or is it wrong to identify an author's character with the author himself?

General Putnam offers a completely different attitude to the approach of death. How do you account for this?

The Italian in England

At the time of this episode Italy was under the rule of the Austrians whose leader was Metternich. The Italian (he is in England when he tells the story) has taken part in an unsuccessful revolt against the Austrian authority and has had to go into hiding.

What happened to Charles, and why does the Italian call Metternich "our friend"? What was it that made him tell the girl the truth?

Do you know of any modern counterparts to this story? In what ways is it good drama?

The Ballad of Culver's Hole
p. 143

This poem—like "The Italian in England"—is about a fugitive, but here one must piece together the story from the words of the pursuers. It has a strange dramatic quality with the dialogue contending with the hissing of the sea as the men call out to one another.

There is some surprising and evocative language ("Voices like claws are closing in"), and a strange sense of foreboding and danger ("The dark is helping the digging mole/To cut our exit off").

Index of First Lines

Index of Authors

Acknowledgements

For permission to reprint copyright material grateful acknowledgements are due to Adrian Henri and Rapp & Whiting Ltd. for "Tonight at Noon" from *The Liverpool Scene*; Roger McGough and Hope Leresche & Steele for "Mother the Wardrobe is Full of Infantrymen" and "A Square Dance" from *Penguin Modern Poets 10*; Peter Champkin for "The Honourable Company" and "Jingle for Children"; Philip Larkin and Faber & Faber Ltd. for "Take One Home for the Kiddies" from *The Whitsun Weddings*; William Stafford and Harper & Row for "Travelling through the Dark" from *Travelling through the Dark*; Judith Wright and Angus & Robertson Ltd. for "Birds" from *The Gateway*; Ted Hughes and Faber & Faber Ltd. for "A Dream of Horses" from *Lupercal*, and "Two Wise Generals" from *The Hawk in the Rain*; Edwin Muir and Faber & Faber Ltd. for "The Horses" and "The Castle" from *Collected Poems*; Hubert Nicholson for "The Man in the Bowler Hat" by A. S. J. Tessimond; W. H. Auden and Faber & Faber Ltd. for "The Unknown Citizen", "As I Walked Out One Evening" and "Roman Wall Blues" from *Collected Shorter Poems 1927–1957*; A. P. Watt & Son and Robert Graves for "Lollocks" from *Collected Poems*; Norman MacCaig and The Hogarth Press Ltd. for "Spate in Winter Midnight" from *A Common Grace*; Laurence Pollinger Ltd. and the Estate of the late Mrs. Frieda Lawrence for "On the Balcony" from *The Complete Poems of D. H. Lawrence*; Constable & Co. Ltd. for "Li Fu-Jen" from *170 Chinese Poems* by Arthur Waley; Vernon Scannell for "A Case of Murder" from *Walking Wounded*; F. L. Lucas and The Bodley Head for "Spain, 1809" from *From Many Times and Lands*; Mary Gilmore and Angus & Robertson Ltd. for "Nationality"; Charles Causley and Rupert Hart-Davis Ltd. for "Innocent's Song" and "I am the Great Sun"; Penguin Books Ltd. for "The Schoolmaster" from *Yevgeny Yevtushenko—Selected Poems*; Dannie Abse and Hutchinson & Co. Ltd. for "The French Master" from *Golders Green* and "Emperors of the Island" from *Tenants of the House*; Harold Owen and Chatto & Windus Ltd. for "Futility" and "The Chances" from *The Collected Poems of Wilfred Owen*; G. T. Sassoon for "Attack" and "Everyone Sang" by Siegfried Sassoon; Holt, Rinehart & Winston Inc. for "Grass" from *Cornhuskers* by Carl Sandburg; Routledge & Kegan Paul Ltd. for "War Poet" from *Collected Poems of Sidney Keyes*; Keith Douglas and Faber & Faber Ltd. for "Enfidaville" from *Collected Poems*; Edgell Rickword for "The Soldier Addresses his Body"; Zofia Ilinska for "Aikichi Kuboyama"; Scorpion Press for "Your Attention Please" by Peter Porter; Thomas Blackburn for "Bombs" and "A Point of Honour"; the Trustees of the Hardy Estate, and Macmillan & Co. Ltd. for "A Trampwoman's Tragedy", "The Convergence of the Twain"